C H I N A

PAKISTAN

NEPAL

BHUTAN

BANGLADESH

Jammu Tawi

Pathankot
Amritsar   Joginder Nagar
            Simla
Kalka
Bhatinda   Chandigarh
Sri Ganga Nagar   Hisar   Moradabad   Kathmandu
Bikaner   Jind   DELHI   Bareilly   Gonda   Gorakhpur   Raxaul   Jaynagar   Darjeeling   Siliguri
           Rewari   Mathura   Faizabad   Muzaffarpur
                     Agra   Lucknow   Mau   Chhapra   Katihar
Jaipur   Bandikui   Kanpur   Fatuha
Jaisalmer   Dhaulpur   Allahabad   Patna
          Ajmer   Gwalior
Jodhpur   Sawai Madhopur   Jhansi   Varanasi   Chittaranjan
                           Orchha   Dehri-on-Sone   Dhanbad   Shantipur
Chittaurgarh   Kota
Barmer   Udaipur   CALCUTTA
                         Sanchi
Mahesana   Bhopal   Jabalpur
Morbi   Ahmedabad   Ujjain
Vadodara   Dabhoi   Itarsi
Porbandar   Dongargarh
         Surat
Bhavnagar   Nagpur
              Murtajapur

BAY
OF BENGAL

BOMBAY   Waltair
Matheran   Latur
     Pune   Kurduwadi   Secunderabad   Rajahmundry
         Miraj   Hyderabad
Kolhapur   INDIA
         Belgaum   Vijayawada
Vasco-da-Gama   Hubli   Guntakal

ARABIAN SEA

         Bhadravati
                    Bangalore
         Arsikere   Madras
              Mysore   Salem   Villupuram
                   Ooty   Tiruchchirappalli
              Mettuppalaiyam
Cochin
Alleppey   Periyar   SRI
Quilon   LANKA
Trivandrum
    Kanniya Kumari

APPROXIMATE SCALE

0   50   100   200   300   400   500 Miles

0   100   200   400   600   800 Kilometres

INDIAN OCEAN

To Linda, Jill and Lyn for their tolerance!

INDIA
'No problem Sahib!'

by Peter Jordan
Richard Paget and David Charlesworth

1

CONTENTS

LOCOMOTIVE CLASSES • PLATE NUMBERS

Broad-gauge
WP : 4, 7, 8, 18, 19, 26, 29, 50, 66, 70, 97, 98, 142, 206, 207, 210, 256, 259, 264
WG : 8, 24, 34, 87, 91, 96, 99, 151, 209, 210, 254, 257, 262
WL : 249, 266
XA : 162
XD : 110
AWC : 94
AWD : 161
CWD : 10, 34
HPS : 25, 34, 93, 96
HSM : 82
WDM1 : 69
WDM2 : 6, 59, 111, 146, 149, 208, 221
WDM4 : 39
WDS4 : 222
WDS6 : 27
WAP1 : 3
WAM1 : 265
WAM2 : 81
WAM4 : 180, 258
WCM1 : 164
WCM2 : 157
WCM4 : 163
WCM5 : 165

WCG1 : 158, 159, 160, 165
WCG2 : 171, 173, 175
WCAM1 : 179
EMU : 79, 154, 168
Metre-gauge
YP : 5, 16, 33, 40, 46, 49, 55, 59, 61, 67, 90, 120, 124, 125, 137, 140, 225
YG : 2, 15, 21, 38, 47, 58, 86, 123, 125, 139, 263
YL : 48, 119, 243
YB : 181
YD : 127, 130, 131, 133, 134, 136
WD : 230
T : 35
X : 101, 104
E : 117, 118
YDM1 : 89
YDM4 : 9, 22, 122, 240
YRD1 : 36
YAM1 : 95
EMU : 92
Narrow-gauge
ZB : 183, 184, 186, 188, 193, 196
CS : 83
ZA/3 : 244

ES : 115
W : 202
W1 : 196
WT : 189
P : 198
B : 197
K : 194, 195
G : 138
BC : 141
ML : 143
B/DHR : 72, 74, 75
ND : 214, 217
NM : 211, 212
NH/2 : 218
NH/3 : 218
NH/4 : 214
NH/5 : 215, 216
ZDM2 : 252
NDM1 : 144
NDM5 : 219, 220
Other lines
BPT : 155, 156
Martins : 57
Industrial : 60, 61, 62, 64, 65
Nepal Rly : 52, 53, 54

LOCOMOTIVE BUILDERS

Ajmer : Indian Railways, Bombay Baroda & Central India Railway
Sir W G Armstrong Whitworth & Co., Newcastle-upon-Tyne, U.K.
Avonside Engine Co. Ltd., Bristol, U.K.
W G Bagnall Ltd., Stafford, U.K.
Baldwin Locomotive Works, Philadelphia, U.S.A.
Canadian Locomotive Co. Ltd., Kingston, Ontario, Canada
Chittaranjan Locomotive Works, Chittaranjan, West Bengal
Fabryka Locomotywim Chrzanow, Poland
Corpet Louvet & Cie., Courneuve, Seine, France
Henschel & Sohn, Kassel, West Germany
Hitachi Ltd., Japan
Hudswell, Clarke & Co. Ltd., Leeds, U.K.
Hunslet Engine Co. Ltd., Leeds, U.K.
Kerr, Stuart & Co. Ltd., Stoke-on-Trent, U.K.
Krauss-Maffei AG, Munchen-Allach, West Germany

Manning, Wardle & Co. Ltd., Leeds, U.K.
Mitsubishi Heavy Industries Ltd., Japan
Nasmyth, Wilson & Co. Ltd., Manchester, U.K.
Neilson & Co., Glasgow, U.K.
Nippon Sharyo Seizo Kaisha Ltd., Japan
North British Locomotive Co. Ltd., Glasgow, U.K.
Orenstein & Koppel, Berlin-Drewitz, Germany
Sharp, Stewart & Co. Ltd., Manchester and Glasgow, U.K.
Schweizerische Lokomotiv-und Maschinenfabrik, Winterthur, Switzerland
Tata Engineering & Locomotive Co. Ltd. (Telco), Jamshedpur, Bihar
Vulcan Foundry Ltd., Newton-le-Willows, U.K.
Weiner Lokomotivfabrik-AG, Wien-Floridsdorf, Austria
Yorkshire Engine Co. Ltd., Sheffield, U.K.

Title page: At Lucknow, a Canadian-built metre-gauge CWD simmers gently (February 1983).
Page 4: Guntakal's metre-gauge pilot, a YG, backs through the station (December 1985).

Three Counties Publishing
151 Moorland View Road, Walton, Chesterfield, Derbyshire
S40 3DD, U.K.

Published 1989 by Three Counties Publishing
© P K Jordan, R J Paget, D Charlesworth

Designed and produced by David Charlesworth

British Library Cataloguing in Publication Data
Jordan, Peter Kenneth, *1948–*
    India – no problem, Sahib ... a tour of India and her railways.
    1. India (Republic). Description & travel
    I. Title   II. Paget, Richard   III. Charlesworth, David
    915.4'0452

ISBN   0-9514916-0-1

Introduction

Bombay's Parel Works on the Central Railway housed the last remaining XA class locomotives in India, fine Pacific engines designed and built in Britain in the 1930's. Photography is totally prohibited inside the locomotive works, so an approach was made to the Chief Mechanical Engineer of the Central Railway, who said "No problem! Although you may not take photographs inside my works, I will arrange for the locomotive to be brought outside for you". He was as good as his word.

This little story illustrates well the warmth of the welcome that any visitor will receive in this marvellous country. Although the bureaucracy seems to be designed to frustrate whatever one wishes to do, there will always be help at hand - someone who will say "No problem, sahib!" and outline a method by which one's wishes, and the requirements of the regulations, can be reconciled.

India has always been a mysterious, magical country to Western eyes, and its increasing popularity as a holiday destination reflects its attraction for the historian as well as the sunseeker. The temples and monuments are legendary, and the beaches at Colva are the equal of any in the world. In addition, there is ski-ing in Kashmir, many and varied wild life reserves, plus the hill-stations retaining much of the atmosphere of the British Raj: all in all, it is a wonderful place to visit.

The transport organisation of India seems to defy all known physical laws: whatever system is selected, it appears that most of India's 700 million population are trying to share the same conveyance. Leaving aside Indian Airlines, the internal air service, operating with modern Boeing and Airbus jets, long-distance transport means either coaches or railways. Urban transport is varied, with taxis, autorickshaws, cycle rickshaws, buses and trams all trying to cope with the vast numbers of travellers.

The long-distance coaches vary between unroadworthy trucks with seats to vehicles with tinted windows, air-conditioning and (ear-splitting) videos. They share the overcrowding common to all forms of transport. The railways provide the most civilised way to travel, at least in the upper classes.

An autorickshaw is a three-wheeled bubble-shaped contrivance, based on a Lambretta motor scooter and, whilst designed for two passengers, is often seen carrying six or eight. It shares with taxis (usually painted black with a yellow roof) the distinction of carrying a meter to calculate the fare. However, finding either with a working meter is, in some areas, a great achievement. The rules of operation, shared with cycle rickshaws, involve the negotiation of the fare for the journey before actually boarding the vehicle. The only problem is that the driver (or pilot, as he is sometimes known in Lucknow) has far more experience of raising prices for Western visitors than has the visitor in negotiating fares downward!

In the smaller towns, the cycle rickshaw is the nicest way of getting about: a fifteen minute ride should only cost about Rs 8/- (and this allows for the negotiated surcharge) and provides a viewpoint from which to observe the steady moving pageant of Indian life en route to one's chosen destination. Bus usage is an acquired taste, and requires prior knowledge of the routes served, but trams, now only surviving in Calcutta, are a real joy - except in the rush hours!

INDIA'S RAILWAYS

India boasts the second largest railway system in the world, covering the country from Jammu Tawi in the north to Kanniya Kumari, the southernmost tip of India. The main lines are usually broad-gauge, with 5'6" between the rails, but there is an extensive metre-gauge system with twenty-four hour journeys available behind steam power, if one chooses one's train with care. There are still a dozen or so areas served by narrow gauge, either 2'6" or 2'.

It is on the trains that a visitor can combine viewing the Indian countryside, especially the villages, with meeting and talking with fellow travellers. As one might expect, there is a choice of classes. Full air-conditioned class, only available on relatively few long-distance trains, gives luxury comparable with first class travel in Europe: crisp white

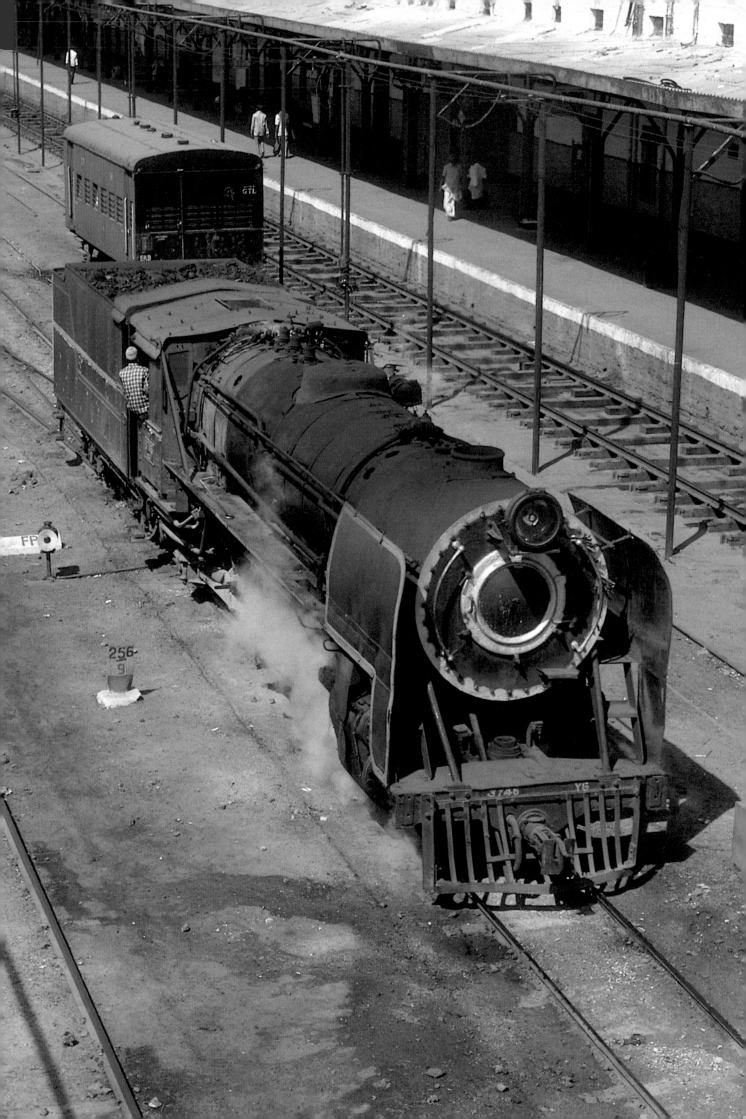

sheets, blankets, and an ambient temperature in the low 60's, more a necessity than a luxury in the hot summer months. Next down is first class, which gives spacious compartments seating six during the day, and with fold down bunks to sleep four at night. For the railway enthusiast, to be able to sit on the step of an open doorway a few feet from a steam engine blasting through desert or mountain is an exhilarating experience. Indian Railways have now realised that the custom offering for their first class outstrips demand, and have introduced an air-conditioned second class at the same fares. This allows double the number of passengers to be carried, and gives the passenger the advantage of air-conditioning, but at the expense of space - and, of course, there is no sitting on the step! The second class offers a variety too - reserved or unreserved, two-tier or three-tier sleepers, chair cars, and so on. Second class has (as a rule) plain wooden seats, and is endured rather than enjoyed.

For the traveller who requires luxury and attentive service, Indian Railways operate the 'Palace on Wheels', a complete luxury train composed of the renovated private carriages of various Maharajahs. This runs regularly from Delhi, visiting Agra, Jaipur and other Rajasthani cities. At least part of the journey is steam-powered.

Before travelling, one is invariably involved with the intricacies of the reservation system. At major stations, one finds large panels containing vast numbers of tiny red and green lights, or, at the least, a panel with red and green discs. These show the reservation situation for the coming month for each of the express trains serving that particular station: red indicates that the train is full, green that berths are available. Red tends to predominate. For any long-distance first class travel, a reservation is essential: the reservation office is invariably crowded, and a completed reservation form showing the name, sex and age of each traveller must be presented to the clerk for each leg of the proposed journey. Assuming the reservation is accepted, the travellers' names are entered in huge ledgers, and eventually, on the day of travel, the names will appear on the reservation list which will be stuck firmly to the side of the coach.

Should the train on which one wishes to travel be shown as full, then the time has come to try alternative strategies to ensure a berth for an overnight journey: approaching the Chief Reservation Officer is a good start, politely enquiring whether there is a 'tourist quota' on the train concerned. If unsuccessful, there is the 'VIP quota' to be explored. For one journey, one of the authors managed to utilise a compartment reserved for the Minister of Food, who, in fact, was not travelling.

Any foreign visitor is fortunate in being able to purchase an Indrail Pass which allows travel on any train, subject to obtaining any necessary reservations (at no extra charge). For a fifteen day first class pass, the cost (in 1989) was a very reasonable US$115 (about £75). It is advisable to plan a tour of India in some detail well in advance, and with an Indrail pass, it is possible to make reservations up to a year in advance - a sure way of beating the queue.

However, if all else fails, a berth can sometimes be obtained by offering a little baksheesh to the train conductor!

Deciding which train to travel on is perhaps a little easier than one would imagine. Each and every train in India is numbered, and many of the expresses are also named. The locomotives of the expresses carry a headboard giving both the name and the number, and all important stations have a departure board giving details of the train, the timing, and the departure platform. In addition, the reservation sheets posted to the side of the carriages also carry the train number. Most Indian railway staff deal in train numbers; the enquiry "Where does the Bombay train depart from?" may well be met a blank stare. However, "Which platform for 6 Up Punjab Mail?" is much more likely to elicit the required information.

There is never any need to go thirsty or hungry on any Indian railway journey. Even long-distance expresses stop for twenty to thirty minutes every few hours, usually at major junction stations. No sooner has the train come to rest than purveyors of tea, coffee, snacks, toys, books and other assorted ephemera descend on it, all loudly proclaiming their wares. One of the abiding memories of overnight travel is of being awoken in the small hours by the cry of "Chai, chai" from the tea seller.

In the north of the country, chai is the staple drink. For a couple of pence, a scalding hot cup of milky fluid is forthcoming, but it seems to bear little resemblance to tea as normally drunk in Britain. However, on a chilly morning, after a dusty overnight trip, it is the liquid par excellence for separating one's tongue from the roof of the mouth. We have a sneaking suspicion that the recipe for chai runs something like this: take two thirds of a bucket of water, and fill it with buffalo milk; then add four pounds of sugar and a quarter of a pound of tea dust; light a fire underneath, and boil for two days; serve whilst hot! Joking apart, providing one does not make a direct comparison with British tea, it is a most refreshing drink.

For delicate Western stomachs, it is perhaps wise to be a little more circumspect with food from itinerant sellers. Although delicious spicy samosas and other tasty snacks may well be on offer, it is better to restrict one's purchases to the plentiful bananas and the sweet juicy loose-skinned oranges. On the expresses, first class passengers will find the train conductor requesting their orders for breakfast, lunch and dinner. Breakfast is usually an omelette with onions, plus bread, curd and jam with a pot of tea or coffee. Lunch and dinner consist of a tray of curry with rice, pickles and chappattis.

All stations boast waiting rooms in some profusion, upper-class gentlemen's waiting room, second class reserved ladies waiting room, and so on. The cleanliness and facilities vary, but in them all, passengers will be found enjoying a snooze whilst awaiting their trains. Some of the better ones have showers. For an overnight stay, the retiring rooms at main stations can be good value at a couple of pounds for a double bed, private shower and toilet. If one is faced with an early morning departure, they save all the problems of checking out of hotels and finding a taxi to the station.

If a retiring room does not appeal, hotels in India come in all varieties and price ranges. In central Bombay, it is possible to spend well over £100 for a luxury room for the night. Conversely, it is easy, especially in the regional towns, to find clean, comfortable accommodation for under £1 per night. Indeed, in Udaipur, we found perfectly acceptable accommodation at a small hotel for less than the price of a cup of coffee at the city's best hotel.

RAILWAY LOCOMOTIVES

Since the second world war, new classes of locomotive have been logically coded; the first digit is W for broad-gauge, Y for metre-gauge, Z for 2'6" gauge and N for 2' gauge. The middle digit is D for diesel, A for 25kv ac electrics or C for 1500v dc electrics - steam locomotives omit this digit. The last letter is P for passenger, M for mixed traffic, G for goods or S for shunting. For steam locomotives, there is also L for light passenger, and a few more exotic variants. From this code it is possible, for example, to deduce that a WDM2 locomotive is a member of the second broad-gauge diesel mixed traffic class to have been introduced. Steam classes dating from before 1948 regrettably cannot be analysed in this way, but these have (apart from narrow gauge lines) largely disappeared now.

Shed allocations are generally three letter codes, but two and four letter varieties do exist. For example, LKO is Lucknow's broad-gauge shed, whilst CB is Lucknow Charbagh, the metre-gauge shed located in Charbagh, a suburb of Lucknow. Many steam locomotives carry a star or other symbol painted on the smokebox door: from its pattern, it is possible to deduce the home shed, as most sheds have their own distinctive style. On the metre-gauge YPs and YGs, distinctive decorative paintings are often applied to the smoke deflectors; one could identify Rewari locomotives by the flying swan or swallow depicted thereon.

The most common steam locomotives remaining are the WP and WG classes on the broad-gauge and the YP and YG classes on the metre-gauge.

WP CLASS

The prototype WPs were built by Baldwin in 1947, and after thorough testing were found to be ideal for heavy long-distance expresses. A further 300 locomotives were built in America and Canada in 1949. In the late 1950's, another 180 arrived in India from Chrzanow of Vienna, and finally Indian Railways' Chittaranjan Works built 259 between 1963 and 1967, to complete a total of 755. These semi-streamlined pacifics are now restricted mainly to slow passenger services, with only an occasional outing on an express, but they remain as fine examples of post-war steam technology.

WG CLASS

The WG 2-8-2 is the all-purpose workhorse, comparable with the 'Black 5' in Britain. They have run anything and everything from express passenger and long-distance heavy freight trains to humble station pilot duties. The first 100 came from Great Britain (North British and Vulcan Foundry) in 1950, and further examples came from many of the world's great locomotive builders in Europe, North America and Japan, and nearly 2,000 further examples from Chittaranjan brought the total production of these fine, strong machines to 2,450. The final example emerged from Chittaranjan in 1970. These locomotives share the same type of boiler and motion with the WP class.

YP CLASS

The first YP metre-gauge pacifics were built by North British in 1952, and by 1970 there were 871 examples, nearly two-thirds of which were built by the Tata Engineering and Locomotive Company Ltd. at Jamshedpur, with the remainder from North British and Krauss Maffei, plus an odd twenty from Baldwins. These handsome locomotives can be seen all over the metre-gauge network, and are invariably fitted with smoke deflectors: they are attractive, photogenic machines which in many areas, still power the crack expresses.

YG CLASS

At first sight, the YG class 2-8-2s can easily be confused with the YPs as they share the same boiler and motion. The work they undertake, like their WG counterparts on the broad-gauge, covers everything from express passenger to station pilot: indeed, from some sheds, they are rostered on passenger trains indiscriminately with the YPs. America built the first examples in 1949, and these were followed by more from Eastern Europe and Japan, although the Tata company built the lion's share. The final batch came from Chittaranjan; the last example, delivered in 1972, was the last steam locomotive built for Indian Railways. The class eventually totalled over 1,000. Like the YPs, most carry smoke deflectors, but some areas, particularly the North Eastern Railway, prefer to run them without deflectors at all.

BIBLIOGRAPHY

Maps:

Indian Subcontinent (Bartholemew) : a good general purpose map of the country.

Official Railway Map of India (Indian Railways) : obtainable from time to time from Thomas Cook, it shows all lines, distinguishing between broad, metre and narrow-gauge.

Books:

Guide: India - a travel survival kit (Lonely Planet Publications): although primarily designed for backpackers, this volume contains more good practical advice on where to stay, where to eat and what to see than most of the other guides put together.

Steam locomotives: Steam Locomotives of India (Continental Railway Circle) : published in three parts (broad, metre and narrow-gauge), full details are given of all steam locomotives which have run in India since 1948. Now out of print, but available through the secondhand trade, these books are the result of much exhaustive original research.

Timetables:

Newman's Indian Bradshaw (Newman of Calcutta) : Every stop of every train in the country is shown, but it is poorly printed and only readily available in India. However, BAS Overseas Publications Ltd, of Kew sometimes have copies for sale.

Railway Zonal Timetables (Indian Railways) : Each of the nine regional railway zones publishes its own timetable twice a year. These include details of through coaches, reservation quotas and, of course, all train times for their zone. These are only available within India.

Thomas Cook Overseas Timetable (Thomas Cook): Published bi-monthly, this timetable gives the times of the main trains on the main routes in India (and the rest of the world outside Europe).

INDRAIL PASSES – are available in the U.K. from S.D.E.L., 21 York House, Empire Way, Wembley, Middlesex, who will also make (reliable) reservations on Indian Railways

THE GOVERNMENT OF INDIA TOURIST OFFICE – is at 7 Cork Street, London W1X 2AB

VISAS – can be obtained from India House, Aldwych, London WC2B 4NA

PHOTOGRAPHIC PERMITS – are required if you wish to photograph any railway scene in India. Permits should be applied for at least three months in advance of the visit, and application forms, which should be completed in triplicate, are available from the Railway Advisor's Office at India House. The permit should eventually arrive from Rail Bhavan, New Delhi, and our thanks are due to the Public Relations department there for granting us the required permits over the years.

This volume is not intended to be either a history, or even a guide book. Each of the authors, having visited India several times, has found himself under the spell which demands return visits, but India is like that. It has the indefinable mystery and magic that leaves the visitor (rightly) thinking that, even after several visits, he has barely scratched the surface of the country. Like any country, India is its people, and each of us would like to express our thanks to these people, and especially the railway men, who by favours done, food shared or perhaps just a smile, have done so much to make our trips so memorable. We hope this book will persuade others to visit this marvellous country, and we hope that they will gain as much pleasure from their trips as we have from ours.

DELHI

Delhi, India's capital, is really two cities in one. Old Delhi, to the north, dates back to the twelfth century, when it became capital of Muslim India, surrendering this title only temporarily in British Raj days. It is a city of narrow streets, colourful bazaars, temples and mosques. The major attractions of the old city include the Red Fort, a mile and a half long, completed in 1648 and now the setting for a 'son et lumière' each evening. Over the road is one of the most extravagant mosques in India, the Jami Masjid, constructed by Shahjehan during the same period.

The southern part of the city is known as New Delhi, and is relatively modern, having been built under British patronage and completed in 1931. Connaught Place is the centre both for business and tourists. It is a large circular park surrounded by blocks of brilliant white faced arcaded buildings, with restaurants, tourist shops and hotels predominating. Proceeding southwards through New Delhi, one finds the impressive colonnaded Parliament Building, Sansad Bhavan, approached from India Gate, a war memorial, by a two mile long avenue, the Rajpath.

For a new visitor to India, the greenery and somewhat less frenetic pace of New Delhi provides a buffer to the culture shock: this is where most of the more expensive international style hotels are situated. The dedicated Indophile, however, may well make for the cheaper, scruffier hotels in Old Delhi, where the cost of accommodation for a room starts at about £1-25.

With regard to railways, the old city is served by Delhi Junction station, which has broad-gauge trains to the Punjab and across northern India to Calcutta, and metre-gauge services into Rajasthan and Gujurat. New Delhi station, deals only with broad-gauge trains which serve the remainder of the country. Delhi Junction has steam, diesel and electric motive power, and a large locomotive shed, always full of interest, whilst New Delhi shows India's modern image to advantage.

1   In contrast with Old Delhi, New Delhi is a modern city of high-rise buildings and open spaces (December 1985)

2   Delhi Junction, on India's Northern Railway, is an extremely busy station having both broad- (5'6") and metre-gauge trains, with steam, diesel and electric motive power. Here, the YG metre-gauge pilot is marshalling the stock for a late afternoon departure (December 1986)

3   Indian Railways' modern image is well shown by the WAP1 electric locomotive designed for long distance express work (February 1984)

4 Now largely displaced from express passenger duties for which they were designed, the mighty WP Pacifics now operate many lesser passenger duties throughout the country. 7566 blasts out of Delhi Junction on train 1DJ passenger to Jind, a four hour journey of eighty miles (December 1986)

5   However, on the metre-gauge, many express passenger duties are still in the capable hands of steam in the form of the YP Pacifics. Here, the photographer clings to the wall as 2325 blackens the sky with 99 Up, the Haryana Express to Hisar (February 1988)

6   Typical of the modern long-haul express service is 126 Up Kerala Express, seen powering through Hazrat Nizamuddin on the Central Railway main line, four miles out of New Delhi on its journey to Trivandrum, almost at the foot of India, some 53 hours and 1,894 miles away. On this occasion, the train is double-headed by a pair of WDM2 diesel electrics, 17304 and 17661 (February 1988)

7 Dwarfed by the enormous WP, one of Indian Railways' 1.6 million employees rakes out its ashpan, adding to the large piles of ash which threaten to engulf Delhi Junction shed (December 1985)

8 In Hindi 'Vikrant' ('Valiant'), a WP from Saharanpur stands alongside a local WG 2-8-2 on Delhi Junction shed (January 1988)

9 A Western Railway visitor: diesel electric YDM4 class at the west end of Delhi Junction station (December 1986)

10 India's main stations are home to many families who spend their lives either on the platforms or at the trackside. CWD 2-8-2 12487 arrives with a passenger train from Jind (February 1983)

Uttar Pradesh

This northern state has as its capital the city of Lucknow, but many other cities are within its boundaries, indeed the population is greater than that of any other Indian state.

Lucknow, as well as being the modern capital, was formerly the capital of Oudh, and its rulers, the Nawabs, were Shi'ite Muslims. Many fine buildings were built by them, such as the great Jami Masjid mosque, and several mausolea. From the British point of view, interest centres on the Residency, famous for its siege in the 1857 mutiny, its battle-scarred ruins stand today in the same state in which they were left at the end of the siege, and in the grounds are well-kept cemeteries. Fairly close to Lucknow, on the southern side of the mighty Ganges, which flows through U.P. from west to east, is the large industrial city of Kanpur; and in the eastern part of the state, also on the banks of the Ganges, stands Varanasi, or Benares, the most holy city in all India for the Hindus. To see the pilgrims on the banks (ghats), bathing in the holy water as the sun rises over the river, is an experience not to be missed. Close to Benares at Sarnath is the site where Buddha preached his first sermon.

World-wide, the most famous building in India is without doubt the Taj Mahal at Agra, also in Uttar Pradesh, on the banks of the Yamuna River. The splendour of the Taj is constant, although its beauty changes in the different lights of dawn, midday and sunset, however it is probably at its most beautiful, almost unreal, in moonlight. The Moghul emperor Shahjehan, in memory of his beloved wife Mumtaz Mahal who died in childbirth, gave to the world in 1653 one of its greatest wonders, the Taj Mahal.

The Yamuna flows into the Ganges at Allahabad, another holy city where, at the confluence, every twelve

11   *From the Hotel Galaxy at dawn, the city of Agra stretches away to its most famous landmark, the Taj Mahal (January 1980)*

12   *At the east end of Lucknow station, a child is returning home with a bagful of small pieces of unburnt coal gleaned from the raked-out locomotive ash: one of many children who will be found at any large station (December 1986)*

13

years millions of pilgrims converge in a great festival known as Kumbh Mela.

With these large cities, and others such as Jhansi, Moradabad, Gorakhpur, Mathura and Bareilly, one might think this state to be totally urban, but not so; the Ganges Plain is very agricultural, and in the north bordering Nepal are the foothills of the Himalayas.

Having so many large cities, it is not surprising that railways abound in U.P. and the electrified trunk route from Delhi to Calcutta passes through it, along with a vast network of other lines, both broad-gauge of Northern Railway and metre-gauge of North-Eastern Railway. On the latter, which extends into the adjacent state of Bihar, steam is still dominant; at Mau Junction, north of Varanasi, several of the small 2-6-2 YL class engines, now quite rare in other parts of India, are still at work.

13 "Can human hands really have built this?" In the midday light, the reflection from the white marble of the Taj Mahal is almost overpowering. One of the seven wonders of the world, it is a place of pilgrimage which really lives up to its reputation. Imagine the sight, had Shahjehan fulfilled his plan to build a tomb for himself, identical to the Taj, but in black marble, on the opposite side of the Yamuna River (December 1986)

14 Bovine power is still the prime mover for freight in country areas, although pneumatic tyres are (sometimes) in use (January 1988)

15 At Agra Fort Station, in front of the Jama Masjid mosque, YG 3502 marshals the stock for an afternoon departure towards Bandikui (December 1986)

14

15

16

16 Vrindavan is a place of pilgrimage to the god Krishna, and is served by a metre-gauge branch line from Mathura. Here, YP 2165 turns on the triangle under the supervision of the local vultures (December 1988)

17 Agra's other main attraction is the Red Fort, built by Shahjehan's grandfather in 1565. Shahjehan himself spent the last years of his life here, imprisoned by his son, with a view down the river to his greatest achievement, the Taj Mahal (January 1980)

18 A footplate ride is an exhilarating experience with the noise and the motion. WP pacific 7002 is en route to Kanpur from Jhansi (February 1983)

19 Before electrification of the Central Railway main line, Jhansi shed had the reputation of keeping its stud of WP pacifics in excellent mechanical and visual condition to run expresses to and from Delhi, a distance of over 250 miles (February 1983)

17

18   19

20

20   In recent years, India has become a net exporter of food, such has been the progress in agricultural production. Evidence of this is shown by the side of a street in Bareilly (January 1988)

21   One of Bareilly City's YGs shows on its cabside overhaul details, the driver's and both firemen's names and even the name of the Locomotive Inspector, in addition to the worksplate of The Tata Engineering and Locomotive Company. The shed code, also shown, is BC. The side illustrated is in Hindi: the opposite cabside carries the same information in English (January 1988)

22   Some diesels have arrived on the North Eastern Railway metre-gauge system. A heavy freight, hauled by an Indian built YDM4 diesel, arrives at Bareilly (January 1988)

23   Although level crossing barriers are often treated as optional, their eventual opening is akin to the start at Brands Hatch - from both sides! (January 1988)

22

21

23

24

24 *At Allahabad Junction, a WG awaits departure with 3AF passenger to Faizabad Junction (December 1986)*

25 *Once the main express locomotives in India, by the early 1980's, members of the*

HPS class, all British built 4-6-0s, were working out their time on secondary duties from sheds on the Northern Railway. 24435, built by Vulcan Foundry in 1949, runs into Kanpur from Lucknow (March 1982)

25

26 By the late 1980's, WP1 7095 found itself on a similar duty leaving Kanpur for Jhansi. The star on the smokebox door indicates that this locomotive belongs to Jhansi shed: most sheds use some form of star to embellish their locomotives (January 1989)

27 A relatively recent addition to the diesel fleet is the Co-Co WDS6 class, used for heavy shunting and trip freight duties. One such locomotive is seen at Moradabad, pausing near the signal box (December 1986)

28 At Kanpur, a potter is seen making disposable clay teacups for use on Indian Railways. Chai, milky sweet tea, is available at nearly all Indian stations for about 5p per (disposable) cup (January 1989)

29 Although Indian Railways still have much to offer the steam enthusiast, even the more modern standard classes are being withdrawn, and cannibalized to keep others of their class in action. Rows of derelict locomotives can be seen at many sheds: this is Moradabad, as evidenced by the 'wings' on the WP smokebox doors (December 1986)

30 A popular sugary sweet is 'Jalebi', being prepared at a small shop in Moradabad (December 1986)

Lucknow

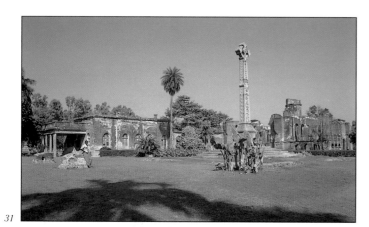

Lucknow, a city of nearly a million people on the banks of the Gomti River, is the capital of Uttar Pradesh, and in the opinion of one of the authors at least, is a very pleasant place in which to spend a few days, both for general interest and railwaywise. It is a mainly Moslem city with a large impressive mosque, a century-old clock-tower, and several ornate mausolea of former Nawab rulers. However for the British visitor the Residency will be of most interest. Built at the beginning of the nineteenth century, it was the scene of the siege of Lucknow in the 1857 mutiny in which about two thousand people were killed, including the commander, Sir Henry Lawrence. Nevertheless it was not taken, and remains today in the battle-damaged state in which it was left. Now it is a peaceful and emotive place, set in lovely gardens on a hill, with a quiet and well-kept cemetery, such as might be found in rural England, and here one can wander between the tombstones and reflect upon the rights and wrongs, the sadnesses and the glories of the British Raj.

Another quiet escape from the city's bustle can be enjoyed by taking a walk beside the river, where buffalo graze peacefully and many birds are to be seen. Especially common are the small, white, heron-like egrets standing in the shallow water near the banks.

For the railway enthusiast, Lucknow is hard to beat. On the Northern Railway broad-gauge diesels of classes WDM2 and WDM4 are to be seen, here being one of the best centres for the latter class. Steamwise, WGs shunt the extensive yards, and, along with WPs, work local passenger trains, and either might be found on the occasional express. At the western end of the main station is the North Eastern Railway's terminus, with both broad-and metre-gauge diesel and steam locomotives.

A few hours spent wandering the tracks at one or other end of the station is very rewarding: one becomes hot, tired, thirsty and very dirty, but as the sun sets when the domes of the station are silhouetted against the evening sky, and a mighty WP throws a cloud of black smoke skyward, one is overcome with elation and returns to one's hotel bodily weary but mentally uplifted. After a cool drink, a shower and change of clothing, it is a wonderful thing to relax and reflect upon the many happenings of the day.

31   The Residency at Lucknow (February 1988)

32   The impressive Moghul-style station buildings at Lucknow Junction reflect the importance of this city as a railway centre. The bicycle is a major form of transport here (January 1980)

33   A North Eastern Railway YP leaves Lucknow Junction with 26 Down express to Mailani: by 1987 this train was running through to Mathura Junction (February 1983)

34

35

36

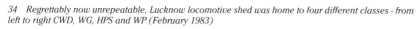

37

34   Regrettably now unrepeatable, Lucknow locomotive shed was home to four different classes - from left to right CWD, WG, HPS and WP (February 1983)

35   Despite the rarity of railcars in India, a metre-gauge YRD1 leaves Lucknow Junction en route to Kanpur (February 1983)

36   On the metre-gauge, a 1938 T class 2-6-2 tank acted as Lucknow station pilot. This engine is now preserved at Izzatnagar Works, Bareilly, bearing the name 'Bobby' (January 1980)

37   Not so rare is the permanent way Inspector's trolley. Motive power is manual (December 1986)

38   The Lucknow metre-gauge locomotive shed is Charbagh, where YG 3362 is resting. In this area of the North Eastern Railway many of the YGs run without smoke deflectors (January 1980)

38

39

39   A speciality of the Mughal Sarai to Punjab line is the WDM4 diesel electric, used for both express passenger and heavy freight work. An express leaves Lucknow for the Punjab and it is surprising to see two freight wagons marshalled behind the first passenger coach (January 1989)

40   Near Allahabad, Jhusi sees two YPs crossing. 30 Down, the Bhagirathi Express from Allahabad to Chhapra in the charge of 2607 waits for 2757 hauling 29 Up, the same train in the opposite direction (January 1989)

40

41

42

43

44

41, 42   The banks of the Ganges at Varanasi are the scene of great activity at all times of day. There are burning ghats, bathing ghats and dhobi (washing) ghats, all of which are kept busy. The morning sun shows this historic background at its best (February 1988)

43   On the outskirts of Varanasi, a YP crosses the Varuna River near the end of its journey with 33 Up Link Express from Bhatni (January 1989)

44   Sunrise over the River Varuna, a tributary of the Ganges, at Varanasi (January 1989)
Mrs M. G. Paget

45   Dawn on the Ganges (February 1988)

46   Amongst the jungle of poles, a YP passes a pond as it runs backwards to Varanasi City station (February 1988)

47   A YG on a freight train, doing precisely the work for which it was designed. 4393 blows off as it enters Varanasi Junction (January 1989)

48   Mau Junction is home to a fleet of light YL 2-6-2s, and one example struggles away with its six-coach train for Ballia. These locomotives, formerly widespread, are becoming rare, as they are underpowered for the work demanded of them (January 1989)

45

46

47

48

21

49

49   The lower quadrant wooden-posted semaphore signal approves the departure
from Mau Junction of YP 2633 with 255 Up Bhatni to Varanasi passenger (January
1989)

50   Gorakhpur is the headquarters of the North Eastern Railway. Until recently, it was

totally metre-gauge, but work is afoot to convert the whole of its main line from
Lucknow to Katihar to broad-gauge. Most of this work is already completed, and
Gorakhpur sees WP 7651 from Sonpur shed arriving with 505 Up express from Barauni
to Kanpur. 7651 will be serviced and turned at Gorakhpur for its return working, and
the express will continue behind diesel power as far as Lucknow (January 1989)

50

51

NEPAL

If India provides the contrasts of experience, then Nepal provides the real contrasts of terrain. Less than one hundred miles separate the Terai, or lowlands, at 200 feet above sea level from the world's highest mountain at over 29,000 feet. However, from parts of the Terai, the Himalayas are not even visible.

The people are particularly pleasant and friendly; visitors are rare and, as such, are made very welcome. Conversation will never be forced upon you, but if volunteered, will be rewarded with warmth, particularly from children seeking the opportunity to try their English. The Terai climate, like its Indian neighbour, is hot in summer though comfortable and pleasant in winter. The landscape is flat and very fertile: the area actually produces most of the country's food needs and indeed exports (usually to India) essentials such as rice, wheat and millett.

Most surprisingly this part of Nepal has one of the world's most delightful little railways. The 2'6" gauge Janakpur Railway runs from its Indian border station at Jaynagar through Janakpur to Bizalpura some 50 to 60 miles distant. The line carries some freight and a large number of passengers, especially on market days, when heavily-laden trains take local people across the border to Jaynagar. Nepalese and Indians cross the border freely, but unfortunately this is not the case with foreigners. The border here is officially closed, and at least for the time being access can only be gained by bus from Kathmandu or Birganj, arduous journeys of some fifteen hours on some of the world's roughest roads!

▲ 52

▼ 53

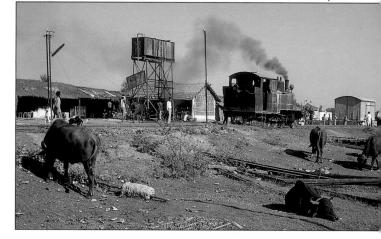

51 A typical village of the Terai of Nepal, alongside the railway (December 1986)

52 The headquarters of the Nepal Railway is at Janakpur, where 0-6-2T 'Chandra', built by Hunslet in 1962 runs round its train (December 1986)

53 2-6-2T 'Rama', amongst the buffalo, prepares to back down to the locomotive shed at Khajuri after having brought in a heavily-laden coal truck from Janakpur (December 1986)

▶ 54 'Surya' leaves Khajuri with what might be termed a well-filled train. There are at least sixty passengers (plus the crew) on the locomotive alone! (December 1986)

Bihar

This state is approximately divided by the River Ganges into a northern third and a southern two-thirds. The capital city of Patna is situated on the southern bank of the river. Generally speaking, it is not an area frequently visited by the tourist, although there are two important religious sites in the state: at Bodhgaya, the Buddha sat under the Bo tree and meditated, and at nearby Gaya is a site sacred to Hindus with temples and ghats.

In the south east, near the West Bengal boundary, there is a major region of coal production centred on Dhanbad, and the Eastern Railway has many broad-gauge locomotive depots for dealing with this traffic. Agriculturally the state is known for rice production, and Patna rice is world-famous. In the north much sugar cane is grown, and this is of great interest to the railway enthusiast since some very ancient steam locomotives are still in use at several of the sugar factories. Also, in the north of the state, the metre-gauge system of the North Eastern Railway is mainly steam operated, and some fine journeys behind the sprightly little YP Pacifics can be enjoyed; for example, travelling from Muzaffarpur to the border crossing into Nepal at Raxaul, and on the Samastipur - Dharbanga - Jaynagar route, although the border crossing here now seems to be closed to foreigners.

In the extreme north-east at Katihar and Purnea, locomotives of the Northeast Frontier Railway can be seen.

Bihar then, with all this activity, is well worth the steam enthusiast's visit.

55   Rounding the curve out of Saharsa onto the Katihar line, YP 2181 leaves a white trail of steam in the cool early morning with 42 Down Janki Express after an overnight journey from Jaynagar (December 1986)

56   Rohtas Industries, a cement company based at Dehri-on-Sone, had a superb collection of fascinating 2'6" narrow-gauge locomotives which worked a line for forty miles out to Tiura Pipradih. Under repair is Rohtas Industries No 1, an Avonside 0-6-2T built in 1902 (April 1981)

57   The last remaining railway operated by Martins Ltd., once of London but now of Calcutta, ran from Fatuha on the outskirts of Patna to Islampur. The power was provided by a fleet of four delightful Manning Wardle 2'6" gauge tanks. No 3 takes water at Fatuha depot (April 1981)

58

58 *After overnight showers, the sun illuminates YG 4334 as it leaves Raxaul with 52 Express to Muzaffarpur, via Sagauli Junction (February 1988)*

59 *Although there is a modern colour light signal and a broad-gauge diesel electric in the background, the old order of power still reigns on the metre-gauge at Siwan Junction as YP 2272 backs to the station to take 241 Up passenger to Chhapra (January 1989)*

59

THE SUGAR FACTORIES

60   The treasure of Bihar! Built in 1873 by Sharp Stewart, 'Mersey' now lives at Hathua Sugar Mills and works transfer freights between the mill and the North Eastern Railway exchange sidings at the station (January 1989)

61   On the main line, 1954 built YP 2272 shows the differences in design over eighty years, compared with 'Mersey', herself a main line locomotive last century (January 1989)

62, 63   Another metre-gauge antique from the 19th century works at Motipur Sugar Factory, near Muzaffarpur. Number 3, an E class 0-4-2 was built as a main line locomotive in 1877 and carries two makers' plates, one from Nielson and one from Vulcan Foundry! (March 1988)

64   In addition to 'Mersey', Hathua also possesses 2' gauge locomotives to work the factory system. With a Baldwin 4-6-0T in the background, an 0-6-0T of uncertain ancestry (but probably either Henschel or Orenstein & Koppel) rests in the foreground (March 1988)

65   Not to be outdone, Motipur also possesses a 1917 Baldwin 4-6-0T! (March 1988)

60

66

67

66   Having arrived from Gorakhpur with train 43, the Gwalior - Chhapra Mail, WP 7154 rests at Chhapra before an unimpressed audience cooking breakfast. 7154 displays the distinctive smokebox style of Sonpur shed (December 1986)

67   The Janki Express, 41 Up, from Katihar and the Kosi Express, 17 Up, from Forbesganj, combine at Saharsa in the evening and run together through the night to Sakri. In this case, YP 2566 has arrived at Sakri with the combined train and has drawn forward to allow YG 3491 to back on to the front portion, the Kosi Express, which is departing for Nirmali. 2566 waits patiently to take the remaining part, the Janki Express to Jaynagar (February 1988)

61

64

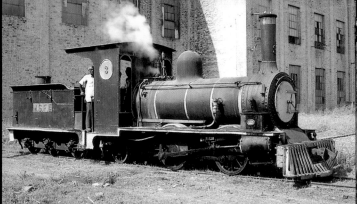

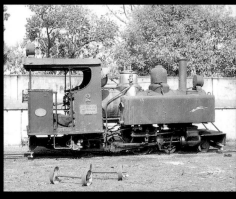

62, ►63

65

68

68   Beside the track at Jaynagar, local artisans complete the manufacture of grinding wheels (February 1988)

69   The first diesel electrics in India were the WDM1s which have a cab at one end only. They are now all allocated to Gonda (although in Uttar Pradesh, still on the North Eastern Railway). They work both freight and passenger trains, and here 17043 waits to leave Chhapra with a westbound freight (December 1986)

70   Sunrise silhouettes WP 7461 leaving Sonpur shed after coaling to work a train towards Barauni (February 1988)

West Bengal

Before 1947, Bengal was centred on Calcutta with its mills and factories, and also covered the jute fields around the Ganges delta. The partitioning of East Pakistan, now Bangladesh, has managed to separate these two complementary functions and has created the Indian state of West Bengal, shaped a little like an egg timer - a wide area around the capital, Calcutta, funnelling down to a narrow strip alongside the Bangladesh border, and widening out in the north.

The partition created a problem for Indian Railways, as the main lines from Calcutta to Darjeeling and Assam passed through Bangladesh territory. The solution has been for a new broad-gauge line to be built northwards from Calcutta, hugging the Bangladesh border for much of its length, and linking up with the former metre-gauge route into Assam in the north east sector of the state.

West Bengal is also home to the holy grail of the narrow-gauge railway enthusiast, the 2' gauge Darjeeling Himalayan Railway. This little line starts from New Jalpaiguri on the plains and climbs to over 7,400 feet at Ghum, a few miles from Darjeeling. Superlatives are inadequate to describe this wonderful railway; suffice it to say that it should not be missed.

72

73

30

71 Taken from Observation Point (named for obvious reasons) in Darjeeling, Kanchenjunga, the third highest mountain in the world at 28,200 feet, dominates the scenery (December 1986)

72 Darjeeling's magic is its railway. B class 'Queen of the Hills', one of a class of locomotives introduced in 1889, proudly displays its maker's plate and nameplate. Twenty four of these locomotives run the railway today (April 1981)

73 The town of Darjeeling clings to a ridge in the mountains. It is a summer retreat away from the heat of the plains and even today retains much of its Raj character (December 1986)

74 In the early morning, the 'school train' departs from Kurseong, bringing the local children (and others) up to Darjeeling for the day. 782 of 1899 blasts out of Sonada with

its crew of six: two sanders on the front, a coalbreaker in the bunker above the boiler, two firemen and a driver. The maximum grade is 1 in 20, and the line is adhesion worked throughout (December 1986)

75 The Darjeeling-Himalayan Railway winds alongside the 'Cart Road' all the way from Siliguri to Darjeeling, crossing and recrossing it for the full distance of 50 miles. It climbs to a height of 7,407 feet before descending gently for the last four miles into Darjeeling. Although the train reaches 25 to 30 mph, the full journey takes all day (December 1986)

76 On its way, the railway passes through several villages, and due to the topography, the line is built through the main streets. Here in Sonada, two locals discuss matters of moment with typical Gorkha houses in the background (December 1986)

74

75

76

Calcutta

Calcutta has the reputation of being the most crowded city in the world: this is hard to believe when looking at the vast green park known as the Maidan, two miles long and over half-a-mile wide. Fort William was built here in 1758 to defend the city: the Maidan was created by clearing jungle to give the Fort's cannons room to fire. It is still a military post. The city stands beside the River Hooghly, which is one of the mouths of the Ganges: the main Ganges delta is in Bangladesh.

The city has two railway stations. The larger, Howrah, lies on the western bank of the Hooghly, linked by an enormous steel cantilever bridge built in Britain and assembled in India in 1943. The second station is Sealdah which is largely populated by electric multiple units, running an intense and heavily used suburban service.

Although Howrah has the glamour of the transcontinental expresses, Sealdah in the rush-hours must be seen to be believed. Train after train arrives in the morning, each disgorging upwards of two and a half thousand people, providing the city's shops and offices with their staff.

77 Constructed as Calcutta's answer to the Taj Mahal, the Victoria Memorial now houses a collection of busts, portraits and paintings telling the story of the British in India. Building commenced in 1906 and it was finally opened by the Prince of Wales (later to become the uncrowned King Edward VIII) in 1921 (April 1981)

78 Calcutta is unique in India in retaining a tramway system to attempt to cope with moving its 9.5 million population. Although an underground rapid transit railway has recently opened, the sheer number of people should ensure that the trams, which have already had a hard life, continue (April 1981)

79

81

79   Another overworked transit system is Indian Railways' EMU suburban service: one such unit, daubed with Communist Party graffiti during the 1980 election campaign which returned Mrs Indira Gandhi to power, runs into Howrah (December 1979)

80   'Pan' is India's answer to chewing gum, and consists of a leaf rolled around betel nut and spices, giving a bright red colour to the chewer's spittle. This may explain the red staining of the pavements (and lower parts of the walls) throughout India! (April 1981)

81   Howrah is Calcutta's main station, and steam has regrettably now been replaced. Mitsubishi of Japan supplied the WAM2 class Bo-Bos, which run many of the expresses here (December 1986)

82   Following the EMU (plate 79), a now withdrawn Armstrong Whitworth 2-8-0 HSM of 1924 draws empty stock into the terminus (December 1979)

83   Some 40 miles from Calcutta lies Shantipur, depot for the little 2'6" narrow-gauge line to Krishnanagar and Nabadwip Ghat. Although now worked by railcars, once these enchanting 2-4-0 tanks (two from Yorkshire Engine Company and two from Bagnalls) had charge of, and were dwarfed by, the trains here (April 1981)

80

82

83

Andhra Pradesh

84

84   Andhra Pradesh has very varied scenery, from the coastal plains to the high Deccan plateau. In the south, near Renigunta, the fertile valley contrasts with the barren mountains (November 1983)

85   The Redcoats are Indian Railways' official porters, and are licensed to carry a headload of 88 lbs. At Secunderabad, an ancient trolley carries a considerably greater weight (December 1985)

85

The state of Andhra Pradesh borders the Bay of Bengal and has Hyderabad as its capital, the fifth largest city in India

Hyderabad is a mainly Islamic city, and it stands inland high on the Deccan plateau, next to its 'twin city', Secunderabad. For railway interest, most attention is focussed on Secunderabad, which has broad-gauge connections to all parts of the country, and an interesting metre gauge suburban service. In contrast, Hyderabad itself is served only by a broad-gauge branch line. In the city lived the Nizams of Hyderabad who, at Indian independence, attempted to create a separate Islamic state. However, this was firmly quashed by the then new Indian government. The two cities are separated by Hussein Sagar, a large water-storage lake, nearly two miles long.

Hyderabad contains what is claimed to be the largest mosque in the world, known as Mecca Masjid, which will accommodate some 10,000 Muslim worshippers, and is built of local granite. It stands beside Charminar Gate, a triumphal arch built in 1591 to commemorate the end of a plague. The views over the city and surrounding countryside from the top of the arch are breathtaking, and available to all upon payment of about 3p.

Andhra Pradesh's coastline is some 500 miles long. At the centre of this Coromandel Coast lies Rajahmundry, at the mouth of the great Godavari River, which the railway crosses by a pair of bridges, each two miles in length. Some hundred miles to the south is Vijayawada, at the mouth of the second great river of central India, the Krishna. On the coast to the north of the state are Waltair and a large port, Vishakapatnam.

86

86   Early morning in India has an atmosphere that is unique. Having arrived in Guntakal with the overnight 222 Down passenger from Hubli, South Central Railway's YG 3730 basks in the sunlight before retiring to the locomotive shed (December 1985)

87   A South Eastern Railway WG rests at Waltair shed (December 1979)

87

88

89

90

88   Hyderabad's Muslim-style architecture is predominant in this view from the top of Charminar Gate (December 1985)

89   The earliest metre-gauge diesels are the YDM1 class, which now work the suburban services from Secunderabad (December 1985)

90   The South Central Railway maintains its passenger locomotives in a very smart green and russet livery. YP 2085 shunts at Secunderabad (December 1985)

91   At Rajahmundry, the Godavari river is crossed by a local WG hauled passenger train (December 1979)

91

Way down in the south of India lies Tamil Nadu, and the slow pace of life reflects the heat - hot in the winter and unbearably humid in the summer. It stretches from its capital, Madras, in the north right to the southern tip of India, Kanniya Kumari, where three oceans meet. There are several cities here well known to the British - Tiruchchirrapalli (perhaps more recognisable as Trichinopoly) and Pondicherry among them. In addition, Ootacamund, usually referred to by Indian and 'Britisher' alike as just 'Ooty', at a height of 7,500 feet in the Blue Nilagiri mountains, is an excellent place to escape the heat and dust of the plains: especially so as it is reached by a metre-gauge rack railway, with fine Swiss-built 0-8-2 tanks climbing a grade of up to 1 in 4. This was where the rules of snooker were first devised, and there are still many bungalows of the 'sound types' and 'good chaps' who ruled India under the British Raj.

Down on the coast, Madras is home to the only electrified metre-gauge railway in the country. Neat little Bo-Bo locomotives haul the long-distance trains whilst silver American-style units provide an intensive suburban service. The British presence here dates from 1653, when the British East India Company built Fort St George, which still dominates the city.

The railways are administered by the Southern Railway, and apart from the all-diesel broad-gauge line from Madras to Coimbatore, all are metre-gauge. Once away from the relatively short electric section, they are worked by smart YPs and YGs sharing duties with the ubiquitous YDM4 diesels.

Tamil Nadu

92   Already well filled, a Madras electric multiple unit approaches an outer suburban station to pick up yet more passengers en route to Egmore, the city's main metre-gauge station (December 1979)

93   In steam days, Basin Bridge was the main broad-gauge shed for Madras. Surviving into 1980, this Vulcan built HPS class of 1950, shows its classic British features: a handsome beast, even in its declining years. The standard coaling method is in use, involving a ramp and several wicker baskets (December 1979)

94 The Southern Railway, due to its distance from the coalfields, has now eliminated steam from its broad-gauge. In happier days, an American AWC 2-8-2 (one of the MacArthurs of the second world war, which served in many countries) rests at Mettuppalaiyam at the foot of the Nilagiri mountains (December 1979)

95 Villupuram, a hundred miles from Madras, is the outer limit of metre-gauge electrification. The Quilon Madras Express, 138 Up, brought in by a YDM4 diesel, is waiting for a YAM1 electric locomotive to back on to take it forward to Madras (November 1983)

96 Madras Basin Bridge shed hosts a South Central liveried WG, while a pair of Southern Railway HPS class await repair (December 1979)

97 On the main line from Madras to Cochin, top link WP 7135 leaves Salem Junction with the Yercaud Express to Erode (December 1979)

98 In superb condition, WP 7491 rests at Mettuppalaiyam between duties (December 1979)

▶ 99 Salem Junction at 6am. The morning light flatters WG workhorse 8989 standing beneath the palms as it is prepared for its day's duties (December 1979)

94

95

96

97

98

100

100   *From Mettuppalaiyam, the rack railway runs up to Ooty. Viewed from the train in the afternoon light, the Nilagiri Mountains show why they are also known as the Blue Mountains (November 1983)*

101   *The rack locomotives that work to Ooty are all Swiss built 0-8-2 tanks. 37389 was one of six built in the 1920's, but a further five locomotives to the same design were added to stock in 1952 (December 1979)*

101

102 Just south of Ooty, the main crops are tea and coffee. The centre of the picture shows the Collector's Bungalow on a tea estate (December 1979)

103 Rack detail on the Ooty line, just south of Coonoor (November 1983)

104 The signal is set as one of the 1952 batch of rack tanks, 37391, begins its descent from Ooty to Mettuppalaiyam (November 1983)

Kerala

105

The south-west coastal strip of India consists of palm-fringed canals and sea inlets, and waterborne transport here is at least as important as railway and road. Part of the magic for any visitor to Kerala is a trip by boat for a rupee or two on one of the regular services between the main towns - it has all the atmosphere of a local bus service, stopping at small hamlets every few minutes. Some canals are up to a mile wide, others only a few feet.

Inland, the main attraction is Periyar, a wildlife reserve based on a man-made lake, where boats transport visitors to watch wild boar and elephants which come down to the lake to drink and bathe. Elephants CAN swim!

Although the capital is in the south at Trivandrum, the main population centre is in the twin towns of Cochin and Ernakulam: Cochin is one of India's largest ports. Fish is an important part of the (largely meat-free) diet here, and the enormous chinese-style fishing nets, standing like dockside cranes ready to dip into the water, reflect the cosmopolitan nature of the whole state. 2,000 years ago, Jewish refugees from Palestine settled here, and have since been joined by Portuguese, Arabs and Chinese amongst others. One quarter of the population of Kerala is Christian, and this was the first area to elect a Communist State Parliament.

The railway is largely confined to a coastal north to south broad-gauge line operated only by diesel power, and a metre-gauge one starting at Quilon, but soon passing into Tamil Nadu, en route to Madras. However, the main line is highly picturesque, crossing wide deep-blue canals and running through groves of coconut palms.

105 Keralan canal (November 1983)

106 At Periyar Wild Life Reserve, elephants gather for their afternoon bath (December 1979)

106

107

107   Alleppey is a typical Keralan market town, with a canal running alongside the main road. A Christian church looks over the scene from the background (November 1983)

108   Most local transport near the coast uses a boat at some stage of its journey. A local cargo carrier enlists the help of the wind to make progress (November 1983)

108

109 The local ferries come in several shapes and sizes, but all share the little cab on the roof for the wheelhouse. The engine lies in the hull, and communication between the Skipper and Engineer is by a system of bell codes, rather than mechanical means. The longer distance boats carry refreshments in the shape of a chai seller who has a kettle full of tea, a bucket of water and one cup and one saucer. Any customer is watched assiduously, and, as soon as he has finished, the cup is whisked away, rinsed in the bucket, and the next customer served (November 1983)

110 Before steam finished on the Southern Railway's broad-gauge, 22474, an XD class 2-8-2, clanks through Ernakulam. The XDs were one of the Indian Railway Standard classes: these were specified in 1924 and the concept lasted some twenty years until the second world war forced India to look outside Britain for new locomotives (December 1979)

111 Beautifully illuminated by the afternoon sun, a WDM2 diesel receives attention at Quilon. On the opposite platform is a uniformed policeman whose socks reach from knee to ankle - they are designed not to cover the feet! (November 1983)

► 112 The State Government Building, the Vidhana Soudha, at Bangalore, whilst appearing to have a distinguished history, was in fact built as recently as 1956. Its white marble dome is surmounted by the Ashok, a three-sided statue formed of the head and foreparts of a lion. The National flag is flying: this is of three stripes, saffron, white and green, with a deep blue wheel, known as the chakra, in the centre (December 1979)

46

Karnataka

113

Formerly known as Mysore state, Karnataka covers some 75,000 square miles in the south of the country. Away from the cities of Bangalore (its capital) and Mysore to the south of the state, it is mainly rural with small-scale agriculture predominating.

Mysore, world famous for the production of sandalwood, is also a centre for furniture. Both in private shops and in government emporia, there is a wide range of hand-crafted hardwood chairs, tables and stools in all sizes, often delicately inlaid, and all at amazing bargain prices, at least to Western eyes. To the south of the city is Chamundi Hill, on which 1,000 steps have been built to allow worshippers to climb to the ornate temple at the summit. On the way they pass the statue of Nandi the bull, carved from solid rock.

Bangalore is now a modern city, although it did exist as far back as the sixteenth century. The Lal Bagh Botanical Gardens provide welcome respite from the bustle of the city centre; a very pleasant place to while away an hour or two in (relative) peace and quiet.

Karnataka's railways are almost all metre-gauge, although the broad gauge has now reached Bangalore from Andhra Pradesh, and work has started to convert the Bangalore to Mysore line. In the north, Hubli houses the locomotive works of the South Central Railway, and Londa marks the start of the branch to Goa, still at least partly the preserve of aged British built YD 2-8-2s.

113 Opposite the Vidhana Soudha are the old High Courts in rich red sandstone. This fine Gothic building also houses the Public Library and two museums (December 1979)

114 Indian station signs are generally portrayed in three languages: the local language (in this case Kannada), Hindi (the national language) and English (being most widely understood) (December 1979)

115 Just outside Bangalore is Yelahanka, the western end of the Southern Railway's only surviving narrow-gauge system, of 2'6" gauge. It runs a limited railcar passenger service to Bangarapet. In late 1979, a surviving Kerr Stuart ES class pacific, 507, built in 1926, rests outside the shed: its sister, 506, is now preserved in a small railway museum at Mysore (December 1979)

116 THE place to stay in Mysore is the Lalitha Mahal Palace, about five miles outside the city. A new southern wing has recently been added to provide international-style bedrooms but the public rooms are in the grand manner: the dining room has a high domed ceiling with stained-glass roof lights (November 1983)

117, 118 At the Mysore Railway Museum is a strange little metre-gauge E class 4-4-4 tank, originally built for the South Indian Railway. It ended its working days at the Visvesvaraya Steel Works at Bhadravati, near Shimoga (November 1983)

119 In Mysore shed, 2-6-2 YL class 5243, built by Henschel in 1956, is under heavy repair (November 1983)

120 Thundering south out of Hubli, visiting Southern Railway YP 2033 lays a smoke screen with 916 Down, the Hubli to Arsikere passenger (February 1985)

114

115

16

117

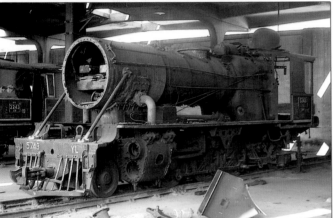

119

118

120

121

122

124

121 The large village of Dharwad has a commuter service into Hubli operated by YP pacifics. The buffalo are being driven for their afternoon immersion in the village pond (February 1985)

122 Heading for the branch down to Goa, a Southern Railway YDM4 leaves Londa with a van train. The locomotive is based at Tiruchchirapalli's Golden Rock shed, some five hundred miles away (April 1986)

123 Standing beside the neat stack of coal, a South Central Railway YG waits patiently at Belgaum for its next duty (December 1985)

124 The 1725 Hubli to Dharwad suburban service hurries through the woods near Hubli in the charge of YP 2767 (April 1986)

125 The Hubli Bangalore Mails meet at Nagargali, between Londa and Hubli. On the right 201 Up, with YP 2848, waits for 202 Down, an hour late, behind YG 3357 (February 1985)

Goa

The former Portuguese colony of Goa, on the west coast of India, really IS all the travel brochures claim it to be - a tropical paradise of blue sea with bobbing fishing boats, endless sand and waving palms set against a backdrop of jungle covered hills. Although sunsets can be spectacular throughout India, here they are particularly so as the large red globe melts into the Arabian Sea silhouetting the dark palms, and all this seen from one of the several small bars built of cane and wood and roofed with palm branches, whilst clutching a cool drink. Paradise indeed!

Yet there is even more than this for the railway enthusiast, since here on the South Central Railway's metre-gauge branch which descends from Londa (on the Miraj-Hubli-Bangalore main line) to the coast at Vasco-da-Gama, British built class YD 2-8-2 steam locomotives are still working. Indeed, except for YDM4 diesels, this branch is the province of the YDs: they amble across the flat coastal plains amongst the palms, and beside the Portuguese built houses and white painted Roman Catholic churches, and they are mercilessly thrashed up the long steep ghat section through the forest, either as train engine or, more often as banker, assisting from the rear a well-filled express or heavy freight heading inland from the coastal port of Marmagao. A visit to Goa is very well worth while!

126 At the end of the day, fishing boats are anchored offshore at Colva (February 1985)

127 At Salcete, near Madgaon, YD 30154 runs between the aerial roots and palms on its way to Marmagao with 291 Up passenger from Kolamb (February 1985)

128 In the jungle behind the coastal plains, Dudh Sagar Falls dwarf the viaduct carrying the line up the ghat to Castle Rock and Londa. In the monsoon season this makes a dramatic sight as the water thunders down (February 1985)

129 The Portuguese style Roman Catholic church at Madgaon confirms this as an ex-Portuguese colony which only became part of India proper in 1961 (February 1985)

130 The Western Ghats form a formidable obstacle to trains running inland, and most are banked up the grade of Braganza Ghat. A YD is doing its stuff at the rear of 297 passenger to Londa (December 1985)

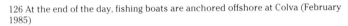

53

131

132

133

131   YD 30165 turns on the triangle in the evening light at Kolamb. Most of the surviving YDs, including 30165, were built by Vulcan Foundry (April 1986)

132   The main industries of the Goan seaside villages are tourism and fishing. The morning's catch is laid out to dry in the village square at Colva (February 1985)

133   YD 30154 is reflected in the River Sal as it heads for Marmagao with a local train (February 1986)

134   30166 stands amongst manganese ore which is ready for export (December 1985)

135   The coast of Goa has many secluded bays, all surrounded by palms - a real holiday paradise. A fishing boat lies on the beach with its characteristic outrigger (December 1985)

136   Showing its sturdy lines, YD 30243 stands at Vasco-da-Gama having worked 295 passenger from Kolamb (December 1985)

134

137

138

139

Maharashtra

Maharashtra is the hinterland of Bombay, on the central western coast, and stretches right to the centre of India at Nagpur, a city noted for its sweet, loose-skinned oranges. It is one of India's largest states, both in terms of population and area. Aside from its capital, Bombay, it contains such well-known cities as Pune (once Poona), both now and in British days an army garrison town.

The cave temples of Ellora and Ajanta, although far from being the only cave temples in the state, are the focus of many visitors. The Ellora site is part Buddhist, part Hindu and part Jain, although Ajanta is pure Buddhist.

The main railways in the area are the Central Railway's two main lines from Bombay, one running north-east to Calcutta, the other south east to Madras, and the Western Railway main line heading northwards along the coast to Vadodara and eventually to Delhi. All are electrified, at least in part.

The real joy for the railway enthusiast lies in two very different narrow-gauge railways. The first is a fairly short 2' gauge line from Neral, near Bombay, climbing up to Matheran and now diesel worked. The second is the famous Barsi Light Railway, running for 200 miles across semi-desert from Miraj to Kurduwadi and on to Barsi and Latur. This was once the preserve of old 4-8-4 tanks built on the principles of Calthrop of Leek and Manifold Railway fame. A journey from Miraj to Latur would take about fourteen hours.

137   Set alight by the morning sun, Miraj's YP 2847 shatters the peace as she climbs from her home station with the 0715 departure, 202 Down passenger to Bangalore (February 1985)

138   Miraj is the southern terminus of the narrow-gauge Barsi Light Railway. G class 4-6-4 shunts tank wagons which act as the auxiliary water supply for the locomotives on their journey to Kurduwadi (December 1979)

139   Miraj is almost unique in having broad, metre and narrow gauge trains. Metre-gauge YG 3455 stands at the head of the breakdown train (December 1979)

140   On Miraj locomotive shed, a YP rests and reflects whilst being coaled ready for a journey south (December 1979)

140

141

143

145

147

141 Nagpur is an outpost of the South Eastern Railway's most complex narrow-gauge system, the Satpura lines, a 2'6" network of over 600 miles of rail. Surviving BC class 643, built by North British in 1909, stands in the sidings (April 1981)

142 Nagpur lies on the Bombay - Calcutta main line: the Central Railway from Bombay here hands over to the South Eastern Railway the line for Calcutta. A South Eastern WP from Dongargarh stands on Nagpur shed sporting the characteristic large tender numerals favoured by this railway (April 1981)

143 The four unique Orenstein & Koppel 0-6-0 tanks which worked the line from Neral to the hill station of Matheran have a system which permits the outer axles to move radially, and side play on the centre axle, allowing the traversing of sharp curves. 738, the oldest example dating from 1905, stands at Neral (December 1979)

144 The steam engines have now been replaced by interesting NDM1 class B-B diesels, which have front and rear articulated sections - not just the bogies move, the bonnets do too! (December 1979)

145 The train starting bell at Matheran. 'GIPR' is Great Indian Peninsular Railway, which lost its identity when the railway system was re-organised in 1951 (December 1979)

146 At Nira, one of the ubiquitous WDM2 diesels heads 308 Up, the Koyna Express from Kolhapur to Bombay (February 1985)

147 From the narrow-gauge line between Miraj and Kurduwadi, these flat topped mountains add interest to the scenery (December 1979)

148 While buffalo cool in the village pond, routine laundry work continues (February 1987)

149 In the midday heat amidst the arid higher mountains on the Deccan Plateau, 307 Down Koyna Express passes a clear home signal. These have three positions: vertical for line clear, 45 degrees for caution and horizontal for stop (February 1987)

150 The south of Maharashtra has many small villages like this, where farmers try to scrape a living from the sunbaked soil (February 1987)

151 A coal train, double-headed by WGs, waits in the centre road of Murtajapur station to allow the somewhat faster Calcutta Mail to use the platform road and overtake it (April 1981)

149
150
151

152

Bombay

Bombay, India's second city, seems firmly of the opinion that it is India's first city. Perhaps its most famous building is the Taj Mahal Hotel, facing the harbour next to the Gateway of India, a triumphal arch through which many famous personalities made their first steps on Indian soil having been brought ashore from their liners. Also, the last British soldiers in India left marching through this same gateway. The hotel still provides a very dignified, cool and expensive retreat from the noise and stress of this very busy commercial city.

Proceeding down Hornby Road, with its arcades covering all types of shop front, one catches a first glimpse of Bombay Victoria Terminus Station, at its northern end. On a similar scale to London's St Pancras, it is a fitting setting for most of Bombay's trans-continental express and mail trains. It is universally known as just 'V.T.'.

The Bombay Port Trust operates an extensive railway system, now largely dieselised, but with some work remaining for the stumpy Nasmyth Wilson 2-6-0 tanks.

153

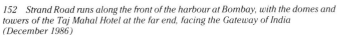

155

156

154

152 Strand Road runs along the front of the harbour at Bombay, with the domes and towers of the Taj Mahal Hotel at the far end, facing the Gateway of India (December 1986)

153 Victoria Terminus Station, pronounced V T (January 1988)

154 Suburban services are provided by these electric multiple units. One runs into Wadala Road Station (January 1988)

155 From further along the same footbridge, one of the Bombay Port Trust's

locomotives busily shunts freight wagons ready for despatch inland. In the background is a member of Indian Railway's dual voltage WCAM1 class (December 1986)

156 A friendly driver pauses to allow the photographer to capture the cabside detail of the Port Trust crest and maker's plate (January 1988)

157 Teatime arrival at VT. British built WCM2 class 20177, dating from 1957, runs in from Pune with 326 Up passenger. This class formerly worked from Calcutta before the lines there were converted from 3000 volts dc to 25kv ac (February 1985)

157

158

The railways from V.T. are electrified at 1500 volts direct current (in contrast to 25kV ac elsewhere), first introduced in the 1920s. Some of the earliest 'Crocodile' locomotives, built by Metropolitan Vickers at that time, still survive on shunting and station pilot duties, and many main line electric engines date back to the early 1950s.

158   Reflecting Swiss development of the late 1920's, many of Metropolitan Vickers' WCG1 Crocodiles still act as shunters and station pilots on the 1500 volt system. These are unusual in having articulated bodies. These locomotives are fondly regarded by their crews, and many bear their original Great Indian Peninsular Railway numbers in addition to their official ones; in this case 4503 is chalked on the bodyside (February 1985)

159   Inside the WCG1 locomotives, the corridor between the cabs houses the pole used for manipulating the pantograph (January 1988)

160   The control panel of the first member of the class, built in 1928, shows the locations of Metropolitan Vickers, Manchester and Sheffield. Perhaps this foresaw the first main line 1500 volt dc electrification in Britain from Manchester to Sheffield, which opened in 1952. The British line has now closed, but the WCG1s soldier on (January 1988)

161   On the Western Railway, steam lasted into the 1980's in the form of American 2-8-2s of the AWD class. Their shed was at Parel where 12715 is on the turntable (January 1980)

162   Also at Parel is the Central Railway's main locomotive works, where the last surviving XA pacifics worked out their days as works pilots. They were built as branch passenger locomotives between 1929 and 1935 (January 1980)

163   At VT's locomotive shed, an Hitachi built WCM4 waits between duties. Dating from 1960, these were the last foreign-built electrics with bonnets (January 1988)

164   British-built in 1955, many of the WCM1 class now carry these colours, almost mimicking BR's Network South East livery. It appears somewhat incongruous on a dated locomotive design (January 1988)

165   Three locomotives at VT. A Crocodile WCG1 lurks behind Indian built WCM5 20090, whilst 20093, another of the latter class, brings in 304 Up, the Mahalaxmi Express from Kolhapur (January 1988)

159

160

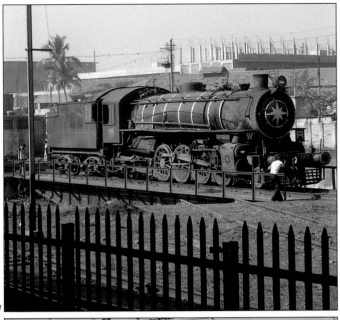

166

167

168

169

166 Outside the suburban station of Mankhurd, the local fish market is in full swing (March 1986)

167 Suburban Indians know within an inch the loading gauge of their railways, and take full advantage of the space outside it. Land is, as in any city, at a premium (January 1988)

168 Many Central Railway suburban trains terminate at Mankhurd where some of the local population exist in housing conditions which illustrate problems not unique to India. A local lad is fishing in the stagnant water - what will he catch? (March 1986)

169 Almost forgotten from a previous era, this signal box remains fully staffed as a ground frame to control the local sidings near Dadar (January 1988)

170 Hornby Road. These Bombay double-deck buses can, in the rush hour, carry around 250 people. They have separate conductors for upstairs and downstairs (April 1981)

▶ 171 The Central Railway's newest class of electrics are the WCG2s, built at Chittaranjan. One example prepares to leave VT with 307 Down, the Koyna Express (February 1985)

▶ 172 Photographic support team! (November 1983)

▶ 173 The ghats. A double-headed freight commences the descent from Igatpuri, crawling cautiously down the grade (January 1988)

▶ 174 In the event of a runaway, ample provision is made to arrest its progress. We would love to see this tested, but from a safe distance! The points are always set for the escape siding until a descending train has halted at the signal box controlling the junction (January 1988)

▶ 175 The tunnels on the ghat sections have been hewn from solid rock and left unlined. The WCG2 in charge of the train climbing to Lonavla is being assisted in the rear by a further pair of the same class (February 1985)

▶ 176 Double heading of a different kind! (January 1988)

170

Soon after leaving VT, the lines to Calcutta and Madras are both faced by the Western Ghat range of hills, and each ascends to the plateau by a gruelling fifteen mile climb at grades up to 1 in 36. For these climbs, fleets of modern WCG2 electrics are available as bankers for uphill trains. To provide additional braking on downhill ones, it is by no means unusual to see three locomotives heading freights, with a further one at the rear.

172

173

175

177
178

This is a mainly lowlying state on the west coast of India. Its greatest claim is that Mahatma Gandhi was born in Gujurat at Porbandar, and from the city of Ahmedabad managed the struggle against the British. Nowadays, Ahmedabad is a large congested city of 1.75 million people involved in the west coast's textile industry. It stands on the Sabarmati River, which is usually dry due to dams and irrigation schemes upstream; water shortage is one of the state's main problems. On the west bank of the Sabarmati at Ahmedabad, Gandhiji's Ashram is situated, a quiet place full of atmosphere, housing a museum portraying aspects of the Mahatma's life, and preserving a room just as it was in his lifetime, including the spinning wheel. For those who admire the example set to the world by this great man, a visit here is essential. Despite Ahmedabad's industry, several other interesting and historic places are to be found: wells, temples and mosques, including Sidi Bashir Mosque, famous for its 'shaking' minarets as a safeguard against earthquakes. The capital of this state is a modern planned city built in 1960, and named Gandhinagar in honour of the great man.

Another large textile city is Surat, and between here and Ahmedabad to the north is the city of Baroda, or Vadodara as it is now called, one of the most pleasant cities of India. This was the site of the palace of the rulers of the princely state of Baroda, the Gaekwars, and there are many shady parks here, one with a miniature railway, and a museum and art gallery housing a good collection of both Eastern and European paintings.

Railwaywise, Gujurat is dominated by the Western Railway's main line from Bombay Central, through Surat and Vadodara to Ahmedabad, and continuing to Delhi. The Kathiawar Peninsula however, in the west of the state, is criss-crossed by metre-gauge tracks, and it was here, especially at Bhavnagar, that many ancient locomotives were to be found until quite recently. Indeed, the British built 4-6-0 YB class may even in 1989 be found at Porbandar and possibly too at Sabarmati Junction, near Ahmedabad. However, it is the state's narrow-gauge systems which attract most interest from the railway enthusiast.

177 *Gandhi's Ashram. Under a portrait of the Indian leader sits a follower operating a similar spinning wheel to that used by Gandhi himself. Beneath the portrait, Gandhi's prayers have been printed (February 1987)*

178 *Looking across the dry Sabarmati river bed at Ahmedabad, the Nehru Bridge leads the eye to some of the modern buildings of this large industrial city. (January 1988)*

179

180

At Dabhoi near Vadodara, the busiest narrow-gauge junction in the world is to be found, with no less than five routes radiating from here. This was originally the Gaekwar's Baroda State Railway, and it has its works at Pratapnagar on the outskirts of Vadodara. Shorter tracks, separate from the above system, are in operation from Bilimora, Kosamba, Ankleshwar, Nadiad, Champaner Road, Godhra and Piplod, at all of which connections can be made with the main line, and others are found in the west of the state at Bhavnagar, Morbi and Joravarnagar. All are currently steam operated, mainly by modern 2-6-2 ZB standard class engines, but older ones survive on some lines, and will provide enough interest to satisfy even the most ardent enthusiast!

181

1

183

179 Indian Railways now have some imaginative liveries. At Ahmedabad shed, 21829 waits in the sun: it is a WCAM1 dual voltage electric locomotive, able to work both the 25kv a.c. main line north from Bombay, and also the 1500v d.c. lines around Bombay and its port. It is one of a class of fifty-three which first emerged from Chittaranjan locomotive works in 1975 (January 1988)

180 Ahmedabad station's inhabitants complete their laundry whilst a pair of standard 25kv a.c. WAM4 electrics, 20527 and 20550, await the road south (January 1980)

181 Recently outshopped, one of Mahesana's smart YB metre-gauge 4-6-0s busies itself shunting by the station. 30015 was built in 1935 at the Western Railway's works at Ajmer, although most of this class were built in Britain (January 1980)

182 It is well known that the chappati is an important part of the Indian diet - even the squirrels enjoy them. It illustrates the principle that nothing in India is wasted! (January 1988)

183 Arriving in Pratapnagar, a standard ZB delays the bicycles with 199 Down Mixed from Jambusar Junction. A total of forty seven of these locomotives were built for Indian Railways in England, France and Germany: 74 is a French example from Corpet Louvet & Co. (February 1987)

184 To the east of the station is the Works, where a ZB is receiving attention. It is capable of all types of repair, from heavy overhaul downwards, and, in addition to its narrow-gauge responsibilities, deals with repairs to broad-gauge stock, for which purpose a branch leads in from the main line (January 1980)

185 Dabhoi is a small city near Vadodara, dating from the thirteenth century, with few signs that much has altered since. The city walls, although partly ruined, remain as a fine example of an ancient fortified city, with narrow streets and a large lake, in which yet more laundry is in progress (February 1985)

184

185

69

186

186   The permanent way staff often live beside the line whilst work is in progress, as here at Kalanpur: in the early evening ZB 69 approaches with 207 Down passenger to Chhota Udepur (February 1985)

187   Legend has it that the intricately-carved city walls of Dabhoi were built in just one day. You just can't find workmen like that these days! (February 1985)

188   A requisite of any visit to an Indian locomotive shed is that all the staff must have their photographs taken. The coaling team at Dabhoi is no exception (January 1988)

189   Dabhoi's station pilot is a WT class 0-6-4 tank, of which only six were built, all by Bagnalls (January 1988)

187

188

189

190

190 *Having spotted the photographer, a shy lady in the yellow sari turns away whilst the others pose for the camera (January 1988)*

191 *'Poterage' rates are quoted in Hindi, English and Gujurati. Most eventualities seem to be covered (January 1988)*

192 *Brake vans on the Dabhoi system contain animal boxes, some with ornate doors (January 1988)*

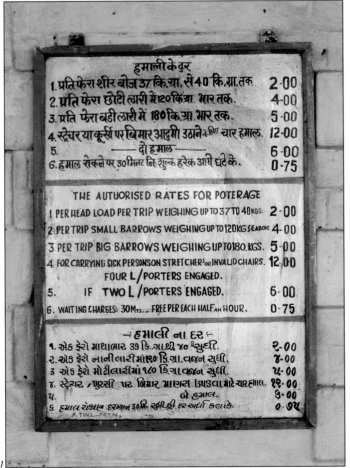

191

192

193   Pride of its shed, ZB 75 leaves Dabhoi with 199 Down to Chhota Udepur beneath the attractive semaphores (February 1987)

194, 195   Pratapnagar Works' regular shunter is the unique K class 2-6-4 tank, 563. Built by Kerr Stuart in 1928, it was specially steamed for the photographers, thanks to the Works Manager (January 1988)

196   Looking more ancient than its 1948 building date, W1 class 593 is spick and span posing outside Dabhoi shed. This locomotive bears Halol's shed code, which lies on a separate line some twenty miles north, and was probably on a running-in turn from Pratapnagar Works after overhaul (January 1988)

197   Surviving into the 1980's, the Dabhoi system had a fleet of seven B and C class 2-8-4 tanks for local shunting: the B's were built by Hudswell Clarke between 1910 and 1912, the C's by Kerr Stuart in 1921. B class 0557 takes water at Dabhoi station (January 1980)

198   Four P class 4-6-0's were built: two in 1929, two in 1949. 605 is one of the earlier ones, with an enthusiastic driver (January 1988)

199   Bemused families view the antics of one of the authors beside the main line at Surat (February 1985)

200   Kosamba shed ashpickers (January 1988)

201   Vadodara's Sayaji Bagh gardens contain a small circular railway with a fine Pacific built by Charles Bullock for the Surrey Border and Camberley Light Railway in 1938 (November 1983)

202   The predecessors to the ZB class for working most of the Western Railway narrow-gauge lines were the W class 0-6-2s, introduced in 1912. 575 stands cold at Kosamba shed (January 1988)

193

194

▶ 195

196

197

198

199

200
◀

201

202

Madhya Pradesh

203

204

This state lies on the central plateau of India, and was historically known as Malwa. Its capital is Bhopal, consisting of a modern part as befits a capital city of present day India, and an ancient part alongside two large lakes: the city takes its name from its eleventh century king, Bhoj who, by constructing a dam (pal), created the lakes. Bhopal is also well-known for its mosque, said to be the largest in India, and in recent years the disaster when poisonous gas escaped from a chemical factory, killing many thousands.

Probably the state's greatest features are at Khajuraho where the exotically and erotically carved thousand-year-old Hindu temples are very famous, and at Jabalpur where the River Narmada flows through a beautiful limestone gorge. Other well-known historic sites in this state are at Gwalior, where the large fort rises above the city, and at Sanchi where there is a fine Buddhist site on the hill above the town. Both of these can be seen from the Central Railway's main line which runs from north to south through the state. At Orchha, near Jhansi but in Madhya Pradesh, a palace and temples are sited picturesquely beside the Betwa River.

The eastern part of Madhya Pradesh contains coal fields served by the South Eastern Railway, but railwaywise it is the Central Railway that dominates this state with the Delhi-Bombay main line, the electrification of which is almost complete, passing through Gwalior, Bhopal and Itarsi. At Gwalior a two-foot-gauge system offers the enthusiast the chance to savour many vintage British built steam locomotives, although in recent months some diesel and even battery traction has arrived. It is in this city that the Minister of Railways, the former Maharajah, has his home.

203 The Palace at Orchha. (It is a live vulture!) (January 1989) Mr S. J. Paget

204 Beside Bhopal station, a local restaurant prepares for evening customers, as darkness falls (January 1988)

205 With ancient temples in the background, whilst picnicking, two Indian ladies show to advantage the beautiful colours of their fine silk saris. The lady in green, alongside her sister, is the wife of a friend of one of the authors (February 1987)

206 After sunset, WP 7397 struggles out of Bhopal with a northbound passenger train (February 1985)

205

206

207

208
◄

209
◄

210

207 WP 7662 looms out of the early morning mist with 18 Up Janata Express (from Jammu Tawi to Madras) at Bhopal. This was one of the last expresses to be steam-hauled on the Central Railway main line (February 1985)

208 Who says steam pollutes? A WDM2 demonstrates incomplete combustion leaving Bhopal on a Delhi bound express. Semaphores are still in control but their replacement colour light signals are already in situ awaiting commissioning (January 1988)

209 An early start for the Bhopal pilot. At dawn, WG 8760 marshalls the stock for a later departure, its smoke mingling with that drifting lazily across from the locomotive shed, away on the right (February 1985)

210 Some are dazzlingly smart, some are incredibly scruffy. One of the latter, a WG, rests under the bridge at Bhopal, whilst behind a less scruffy WP awaits departure for Kota with 94 Down passenger (January 1988)

211 The 2' gauge system at Gwalior has long been a mecca for narrow-gauge enthusiasts. An NM class pacific, 765, built by Bagnalls in 1931, nears the end of its journey from Sabalgarh as it drifts down beneath Gwalior Fort with the morning mixed train, 664 Up (February 1987)

212 Two of the eight NM class spent their early years working on the Western Railway's Ujjain to Agar line, but, on its closure in 1975, they were transferred to Gwalior. One of them, 609, climbs out of the city with an afternoon departure to Sabalgarh, 663 Down (March 1988)

211

212

213   India's Minister of Railways is currently the former Maharajah of Gwalior: his palace is adjacent to the Usha Kiran Palace Hotel, a recommended place to stay, reputed to have been specially built to accommodate British guests, and retaining that genteel atmosphere (January 1988)

214   The cab of Baldwin 2-8-2 NH/4 class 756 seems to be less securely attached than that on the ND 4-6-4 behind it (March 1988)

215   The NH/5 2-8-2s were built by Nippon of Japan, and 813 provides a moving grandstand for two officials. The locomotive is carrying newly-made earthenware pots, presumably for (unofficial) delivery to en route customers (March 1988)

216   Some of Gwalior's stud are now in blue livery, as worn by NH/5 813, on the coaling stage just north of Gwalior station (January 1988)

214

215

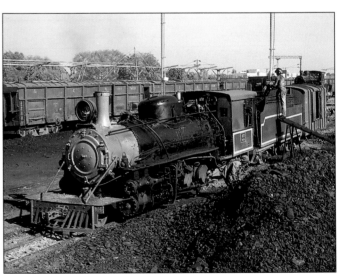

216

217

217 Dating from 1928, the ND 4-6-4s rarely get line work these days, usually being restricted to shunting and pilot duties. Here, 747 has an outing to Sabalgarh, and is caught passing Mahal Gaon (February 1987)

218 In 1922, the NH/2 class from Kerr Stuart arrived at Gwalior, represented by 751 on the right. Behind her stands 755, an NH/3 from the same builder in 1928. These classes were followed by the NH/4s from Baldwin in 1948 and NH/5s from Nippon in 1959 to complete the 2-8-2 fleet of the Gwalior system (January 1988)

219, 220 The new order at Gwalior. 802, named Cheetal, stands in Gwalior station whilst 801, Chandra, is given the finishing touches to its special decorations for the visit the following day of the Minister of Railways. He will be attending a ceremony to mark the introduction of these new Chittaranjan built NDM5 class diesels on the line to Sheopur Kalan (January 1988)

219

218

220

221

223

222

221   To improve forward visibility, a few of the standard WDM2 class diesels have cut-down noses. 17894 roars through Sonagir, between Jhansi and Gwalior (February 1984)

222   All over India, the standard broad-gauge diesel shunter is the WDS4 class, in several variants. Two examples wait in Gwalior under the newly installed electric catenary (January 1988)

223   A pair of WGs on Bhopal shed (January 1988)

224   Bhopal: preparing to take a shower under a water column (January 1988)

224

225   Still one of the finest runs for an enthusiast in India is the full day behind a YP Pacific from Udaipur to Ahmedabad through desert and mountain. 85 Up pauses at Lusadiya (on the Gujurat border), behind Sabarmati shed's 2179 (February 1987)

226   Jaya Stambh, the Tower of Victory, commemorates Rana Kumbh's victory in 1440 over Mahmad Khilji of Malwa. Now you know! This is just one of the features of Chittaurgarh Fort, an enormous site covering nearly 700 acres (February 1987)

225

RAJASTHAN

226

Rajasthan is probably the most romantic state in India. Its very name means 'place of kings', and it is here that one sees India at its most colourful: the landscape is rugged, hilly and with sparse vegetation in the south, and is of endless sandy desert in the north and west. The people wear colourful clothing, especially the ladies, with bright skirts and heavy jewellery, and the menfolk wind long highly-coloured turbans around their heads. Historically, too, the state is colourful, with most cities having forts steeped in history of battle, valour and sacrifice. Such magnificent forts are to be found at Amber near Jaipur, Jodhpur, Jaisalmer and Bikaner, to name but a few. At Chittaurgarh, there is a splendid hilltop fort where, more than once in the past, warriors rode out to certain death, whilst their womenfolk burnt themselves to death in a funeral pyre, rather than be defiled.

In addition to forts, majestic palaces are to be found, and even stayed in, since many now function as luxury hotels. Perhaps the most idyllic of these is the Lake Palace Hotel at Udaipur. It stands like a large white swan in a lake surrounded by hills, and is reached by boat from the old city. As the sun sets behind the mountains, the building takes on a rich orange-red glow and, if staying here, one feels a little like a Maharajah oneself.

The capital of Rajasthan is Jaipur, known as the 'Pink City', where the buildings are coloured pink, and become rich in the light of the rising and setting sun. The main landmark is the Hawa Mahal, or Wind Palace, which is part of the large City Palace complex, and was originally built to enable the ladies of the court, in purdah, to look out on the street below, with its traffic of people, camels and carts, without themselves being seen. Linking Jaipur with Delhi there is a pink coloured train, hauled by a similarly painted diesel locomotive, appropriately called the "Pink City Express". It is most likely the only pink train in the world.

The railways of this state are mainly metre-gauge and steam-worked, and many engines are well-kept and, as befits the area,

229

23(

beautifully decorated, as is that illustrated leaving Jaipur with its chimney bearing a crown. If one travels south from Udaipur towards Ahmedabad by the daytime passenger train (85 Up) one can savour the rugged rocky landscape of south Rajasthan at its best as the little YP Pacific blasts up steep gradients, through cuttings and over ravines among the wild hills.

However, for a really memorable journey try travelling second class on hard seats from Merta Road to Bikaner on a very hot day as the train makes its way through the sand of the Thar Desert. With the window shutters open, smoke and sand blow in, and with the shutters down it is dark, hot and oppressive. Eventually, the odour of thirty-plus people crowded into a compartment designed for half that number, forces those inside to raise the shutters again and suffer the sand and smoke. Despite this, the people, their faces half covered to keep out the biting sand, are happy to talk and laugh with their foreign co-travellers; a musician sings and plays his tambourine with extra vigour at the thought of the many rupees he will successfully extract from the foreign guests! As the sun goes down and camel trains on the distant sandy hills become silhouetted against the orange-pink sky, discomforts are forgotten in the sheer magic of Rajasthan.

227

228

227　The Lake Palace Hotel at Udaipur. It is possible to obtain a double room with bath at other hotels in the city for less than the cost of a cup of coffee here! (February 1987)

228　Near Jaipur, amongst the mountains, lies the small town of Amber. It boasts a large fort, the former home of the Maharajahs of Jaipur (February 1987)

229　Against the Western sky, two of the forest of signals are pulled off to admit 252 passenger from Udaipur to Mavli Junction station. The train will continue to Rewari, where it should arrive some 32 hours later (February 1987)

230　During the second world war, India imported about 270 of these MacArthur 2-8-2s to bolster the difficult metre-gauge power shortage. Known as the MAWD (usually shortened to WD) class, they have survived into the late 1980s as station pilots and shunters, like 1568, taking water in front of the retiring room at Chittaurgarh station (February 1987)

231 Climbing up the 1 in 60 grade out of Udaipur early on its journey to Ahmedabad, 85 Up threads its way through the inhospitable terrain, with YP 2179 in charge (February 1987)

232 Further south, at Rikhab Dev Road, 85 Up crosses its opposite number, 86 Down, here hauled by YP 2640. 2640 and 2179 are two of three specially maintained YPs from Sabarmati shed, kept for this duty (February 1987)

233 Wicked grin at Jaipur (January 1988)

234 The Hawa Mahal is one of Jaipur's main tourist attractions. A cycle rickshaw wallah is hoping to attract foreign custom at an enhanced rate per mile! (January 1988)

235 The booking hall at Jaipur station in one of its quieter moments. Most Indian stations were built during British Raj days to be spacious and airy, largely to provide cool relief from the baking heat outside. However, all too frequently, these halls are absolutely crammed with the local populace, all trying to buy tickets, meet relations, obtain reservations, or just sleeping in the shade (January 1988)

236 Camels are common in most of western and northern India as beasts of burden, working alongside bullocks. Particularly in the Rajasthan desert areas, they have the advantage of requiring a lot less water than bullocks, which need to be bathed daily (January 1980)

237 Just off the regular tourist beat in Jaipur are many little back alleys. In these, India can be seen functioning as it always has, showing little of the special attractions and shops existing just to service the package tourists. One can have a shave or haircut, one's ears dewaxed, one's nose pierced, or purchase any of the necessities of life for just a rupee or two (January 1988)

238 Beggar girl and baby in the Pink City (January 1988)

239 The basis of most Indian cooking is the range of spices used. A shop in Jaipur displays the bright yellow turmeric and red chilli powder, amongst many others. For main courses, the heat of the meal is provided by the spices: most food is served at room temperature. An Indian chef will take great pride in personally preparing and mixing his spices to give a unique flavour to the meal he is preparing (January 1988)

233

2

2

236

237

238

239

240 Jaipur has a splendid array of fine, tall semaphores out on the line towards Delhi. The signal pulled off for 8 Down to Agra Fort is a three position semaphore showing the line fully clear, whilst all the others are of the more usual two position, lower quadrant type. 8 Down is running two hours late, having started its journey in Barmer on the western extremity of the Northern Railway some sixteen hours earlier: the YDM4 in charge is showing every sign of trying to regain lost time (February 1984)

241 At the northern end of Jaipur station, YP 2572 runs in at the end of its journey with 12 Down express from Sri Ganga Nagar. All along the train, milk cans can be seen hanging from the window bars, bringing this vital commodity into the city for sale (February 1984)

242 Inside the locomotive shed at Jaipur, both running and heavy repairs are carried out. As late as 1988, it boasted four different classes amongst its allocation: in addition to the YPs and YGs, there were WDs for shunting and YL 2-6-2s. Jaipur shed is one of the most smartly run sheds in the country. The Hindi symbol on the smokebox door of YP 2842 represents good luck, and is carried by many of Jaipur's locomotives (January 1988)

243 For many years, a 'must' for the knowledgeable enthusiast was the 1700 departure from Jaipur to Toda Rai Singh, 256 Down. Until the track on this line was strengthened in 1988, the YL 2-6-2s were the only locomotives permitted, and a small stud was maintained at Jaipur just for this service of one train each day. With an additional water supply behind the tender, 5132, built by Henschel in 1956, passes under the Ajmer Marg road bridge just south of Jaipur station at the start of its journey. The yellow signals in the background are repeaters for the station home signals. What appears to be a double track line here is in fact two single lines; one is the Delhi main line, the other runs to Sawai Madhopur, and is shared by the Toda Rai Singh trains as far as Sanganer Junction (February 1987)

244 Although 32 miles south of Agra (in Uttar Pradesh) and 41 miles north of Gwalior (in Madhya Pradesh), Dhaulpur is, in fact, in Rajasthan. It is the base for a 2'6" gauge line to Sirmuttra, which has a branch to Tantpur. The line was primarily intended to serve local stone quarries, but it carries a passenger service too. The line is operated by 2-8-4 tanks built by Kerr Stuart or Hunslet between 1921 and 1959, although now assisted by other classes displaced from elsewhere. 735, the oldest tank engine on the line, receives some last-minute attention before going out to work. Two shed staff demonstrate the classic posture of rest, seen throughout India (December 1986)

245 Bandikui, between Agra and Jaipur, has the reputation of maintaining its fleet of YP Pacifics in excellent mechanical and visual condition, with an intertwined 'BKI' on their smokebox doors. At Jaipur, 2683 has taken over 238 Down Bikaner Express to Sawai Madhopur some two hours late and purposefully sets about recovering the deficit (February 1987)

243

244

245
►

Against the Pakistani border, the Punjab bore the brunt of the bloodshed and violence in 1947 when the partition of India and Pakistan saw vast numbers of Hindus leaving what is now Pakistan, and similar numbers of Muslims entering, before the border was closed. Before this, Punjab state straddled the present border, with its capital in Lahore.

Today, the Punjab is known as 'the breadbasket of India', and is the most advanced state of India in terms of agriculture: the main crops are wheat, rice and milk. Its capital is Chandigarh.

The railways are mostly broad-gauge, and reflect the pre-1947 situation before partition. Former main lines which ran across the border to cities now in Pakistan, are truncated to the last station on Indian territory. However, the line across the border at Atari is still open, and daily carries India's one International train, and the green and cream coaches of Pakistan Railways can be seen at Amritsar station before commencing their short journey to Lahore.

Punjab

246

246   The Golden Temple at Amritsar; a beautiful building open to visitors of any religious denomination, but visitors should note that neither leather nor tobacco is permitted within its gates (November 1983)

247   The memorial to the Amritsar Massacre, in the now peaceful Jalianwalabagh Gardens (November 1983)

248   One of the more roadworthy examples of an Indian lorry: all bear the inscription 'Public Carrier' on the front and 'Horn Please' on the rear. Even if the latter injunction is obeyed by a potential overtaker, the lorry will continue its steady progress in the middle of the road (November 1983)

249   For the more lightly-laid broad-gauge lines in several parts of India, the WL Pacific was designed, but these are now only to be found in the Punjab. 15017 runs into Bhatinda passing 15056 at the entrance to the shed (February 1984)

247
◄

248

249

250

Himachal Pradesh

Up in the Himalayan Mountains, Himachal Pradesh has magnificent scenery and clear air. Simla, the capital, was the seat of the government during the summer in British days, when the heat of Delhi became too much to bear.

The main interest for tourists is trekking, nice and easy in the lush Kangra and Kulu valleys, but severe further east in the snowy heights of Lahaul and Spiti where the culture is Tibetan. Indeed, Dharamsala in the north west of the state is the exile home of the Dalai Lama who fled from Tibet at the time of the Chinese invasion.

Much of the state is very lightly populated, due to the terrain, and roads are a rarity, let alone railways. However two small 2'6" gauge railways do exist: the Kangra Valley line from Pathankot to Joginder Nagar, and a spectacular line which climbs from Kalka, on the edge of the Ganges plain, to Simla, some seven thousand feet higher. In the course of its journey, the Simla line passes through over a hundred tunnels.

251

250 Dominated by the very British church on the skyline, the city of Simla descends steplike beneath it (January 1980)

251 The railway to Simla is still partly worked by these unusual railcars. With the morning mail, a twenty minute pause is made at Barog for the few passengers to partake of breakfast in the alpine-style station buildings (January 1980)

252 Less charming are the more modern ZDM2 diesels which now cover all the other duties on the line. They are replacements for older 2-6-2 ZF tanks, which were reminiscent of those on the Vale of Rheidol Railway in Wales (January 1980)

252

253

Haryana

Haryana is a predominantly Hindu state, formerly the easternmost part of the pre-partition Punjab. It shares its capital, Chandigarh, with the present state of Punjab, and is shaped like a letter 'C' surrounding Delhi; therefore heading north, west or south, one passes through Haryana, hence it has an extensive rail network. The Northern Railway has a metre-gauge express from Delhi Junction to Hisar, 99 Up, and back as 100 Down, named the Haryana Express,

and there are locomotive depots at Rewari (RE) and Sirsa (SSA) on the metre gauge, and at Jind (JHI) and Tuglakabad on the broad-gauge. At the latter are to be found very many diesels of class WDM2, with the shed code TKD worn high on their front.

253 At this time, Rewari shed adorned its YPs with white swans on their smoke deflectors, as on 2325, being turned at its home depot (February 1983)

254 A smart WG raises the dust entering Jind from the south (February 1984)

254

...and so back to Delhi

Our circular tour of India now brings us back to our starting point. We hope you have enjoyed the journey but before boarding our plane, let us have another brief look at the attractions of this capital city. From the culture shock we experienced when we first arrived in India, we have now widened our experience, and have seen the 'real India' away from the major cities and tourist traps. After this, Delhi seems to be almost Western!

255   Behind the cycle repair tree, it is surprising what pedal power can move (December 1986)

256   Now electrically hauled, 362 Up, the 0830 departure from New Delhi for all stations to Agra, was once the preserve of smart green and black Central Railway WPs. One wonders how the local population get their hot water for hair washing nowadays (March 1983)

257   In the foreground, packing for fragile goods is displayed - in this case, eggs. The silver star on the WG at Delhi Junction indicates its home at Ghaziabad, twelve miles away (December 1985)

258   Just south of Delhi is Hazrat Nizamuddin: to ease the congestion in the city's main stations, some long distance expresses terminate here. WAM4 20588 heads south with an enormous freight (February 1983)

255

256
◄

257

258

259

259 At Delhi Junction, WP 7563 waits to take over a Punjab-bound train
(February 1985)

260 Two satisfied smiles and two sacks of unburnt locomotive fuel for an alternative
use (December 1986)

261 There is no need to starve on any Indian station. Food and drink of all types is
available at all hours from stalls such as this (January 1988)

260

261

262

262 *A Ghaziabad WG lurks between Delhi Junction station's platforms (January 1988)*

263 *Delhi Junction's metre-gauge pilot, YG 4289, struggles to move a long rake from the carriage sidings (February 1988)*

263

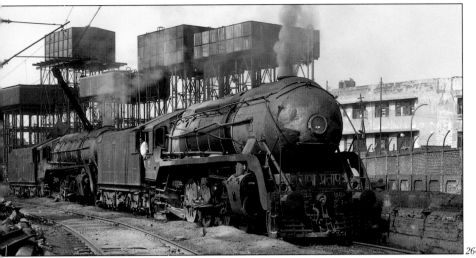

264

265

266

267

264   Steam engines feed on coal and water, and a large station like Delhi Junction will require plenty of the latter, hence the large tanks behind the WPs (November 1983)

265   The first 25kv a.c. electric locomotives in India were the WAM1 Bo-Bos, imported from Europe, illustrated by 20251 at the east end of the Junction station (February 1984)

266   Uncommon visitors to Delhi Junction were the WL Pacifics, which worked in from the Punjab with the Udyan Abha Express for a time.' 15017 stands outside the Shed Foreman's office (December 1985)

267   India possesses a wonderful railway museum at Chanakyapuri, in New Delhi. The brainchild of one of the greatest Indian railway enthusiasts, Michael Satow, it is a tribute to the long history and fascinating machinery that has grown into a system with a prodigious ability to move unbelievable quantities of passengers and freight all over this vast country. The contents are absorbing, from wagon plates to a huge 4-8-0 + 0-8-4 Beyer Garratt, and include 'Fairy Queen', still in working order and dating from 1855, and the unique Patiala State Monorail Trainway, plus a wealth of other historic locomotives - steam, diesel and electric (January 1980)

268   It seems likely that, when this child reaches adulthood, the steam locomotive will have disappeared from the Indian railway scene. However, what is certain is that Indian Railways will continue to serve the country's needs well (January 1980)

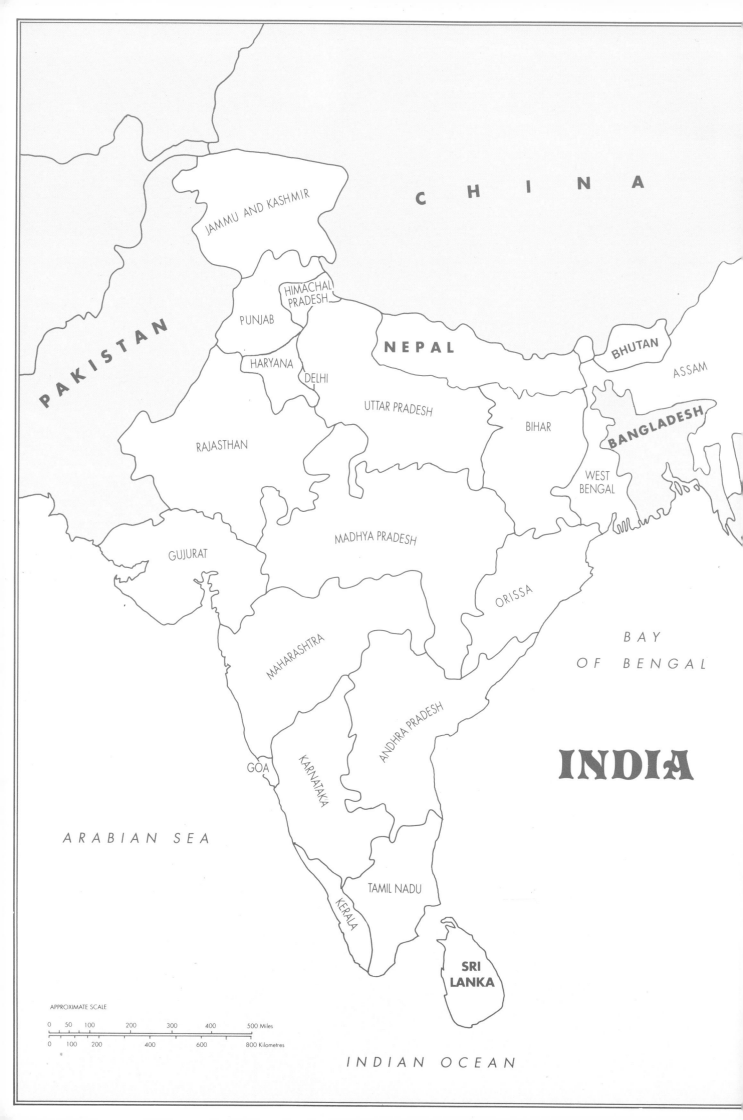